The Politics of Peace

What's Behind The Anti-War Movement?

John J. Tierney

To Herman: Colleague and Friend. Keep up the great work.

Jack

Capital Research Center

About the Author

John J. Tierney is Walter Kohler professor of international relations and faculty chairman at the Institute of World Politics in Washington, D.C. He taught previously at the Catholic University of America, the University of Virginia and Johns Hopkins University. He has held a number of positions in the U.S. Arms Control and Disarmament Agency, including foreign affairs officer in the Bureau of Strategic Nuclear Affairs, division chief in the International Relations Division and member of the U.S. delegation to the Conference on Disarmament in Geneva in 1982-1985. Earlier, he was director of the Congressional Caucus on National Defense in the U.S. House of Representatives. Tierney received a Ph.D. in international relations from the University of Pennsylvania. He has published widely in scholarly and popular journals.

Acknowledgements

The author gratefully acknowledges the support of the Capital Research Center, its president Terry Scanlon and former editor John Carlisle for their assistance. In particular, I want to acknowledge the contribution of Bob Huberty, CRC director of research, who took an obese first draft and turned it into a svelte literary final product. Over fifty e-mails and several months later, almost on time, we have a book!

Nor could this task have been accomplished without the ongoing support of my colleagues at the Institute of World Politics and the students in my classes. I wish to acknowledge the personal and professional encouragement I received from J. Michael Waller and Herbert Romerstein, two faculty colleagues who possess unmatched first-hand knowledge of America's enemies within. A special debt goes to Institute of World Politics president John Lenczowski, whose leadership and encouragement provide the atmosphere where books can be written and lectures presented, and where collegiality allows the human mind to prosper in freedom. Of course, I alone am responsible for the research and conclusions in this book.

Finally, this book is dedicated to the memory of my parents, John and Catherine McMahon Tierney, and my late in-laws, Victorio and Carmela Puglisi, whose generation knew world war first-hand.

Table of Contents

Preface

Like a man in quicksand, my every move to explain the anti-war movement in the United States has drawn me deeper into the subject. Originally intended as an extension of several short Capital Research Center monographs on recent anti-war group activities, this book grew as I uncovered historical linkages in American politics and society that became clearer and stronger upon reflection.

To describe current anti-war protest as a reaction to the invasion of Iraq or an anti-Bush phenomenon is to miss the point. A closer look at the protestors and their associations reveals a pedigree going back at least to the Vietnam era and beyond to the "progressive" and protest politics of earlier decades. Likewise, to view current anti-war activism stripped of its diverse political dimensions—including liberalism, pacifism, isolationism, extremism, communist ideology and the concept of "revolution"—is to lose sight of the movement's background and multifaceted qualities. Current protests and demonstrations, their methods, goals and organizers may appear to be a product of the moment—and even genuinely anti-war—but they most assuredly are *not*.

The leaders of the "anti-war" movement today are leftists in ideology. Almost all oppose capitalism and believe in socialism; many are Communists. At root, they are anti-American rather than anti-war. They may fan out to create a dizzying array of front groups, but this display of diversity is a political fiction. Anti-war activists create a network by moving from group to group, linking generations and causes to one another. They are political chameleons but single-minded in purpose. They split hairs over differences in ideology and fight raging battles over them. But these internal disputes mask a common ideological vision.

Anti-war groups comprise an authentic political movement. They have distinctive forms of organization, outlets for propaganda, favored strategies and tactics, and access to information technology that increasingly allows their communications to be instantaneous and global. In short, they are a political *force,* not simply a school of thought or an unhappy segment of the electorate.

Citizens in a democracy welcome debate and criticism of political candidates. But the anti-war movement has no interest in debate. It doesn't care about George W. Bush; it wants to change the American economic and political *system.* Indeed, far from being anti-war, the movement welcomes "class struggle" that serves revolutionary ends. America's enemies are its allies because the dynamic of politics puts the anti-war movement in league with the forces of international terror. This is not an accusation by the Right; it is analysis from inside the Left, and reflects both the strengths and weaknesses of democracy, the "open society."

In his seminal work on political sociology, *The Open Society and Its Enemies* (1945), the great Austrian philosopher Karl Popper defended democratic liberalism against totalitarian ideologies, including Communism. At the end of Volume II Popper reminded his readers:

> ...the role of thought is to carry out revolutions by means of critical debates rather than by means of violence and of warfare; that is the great tradition of Western rationalism to fight our battles with words rather than with swords. That is why our Western civilization is an essentially pluralistic one, and why monolithic social ends would mean the death of freedom: of the freedom of thought, of the free search for truth, and with it, of the rationality and the dignity of man.

I hope this study of "war resistance in America" allows readers to appreciate our open society and its current enemies. To understand them we must study how they are linked to our democratic society as well as how they are opposed to it. It is with this linkage in mind that I have written this book.

THE "MOVEMENT"

On the evening of June 25, 2004 the President of the United States stepped off Air Force One and entered the tarmac of the international airport at Shannon, Ireland, a country that historically has been one of the most pro-American in the world. But that day and in the days that followed George W. Bush received one of the most hostile receptions any President has received traveling overseas. In what Great Britain's *Guardian* newspaper described as "the most unwelcome American ever to set foot on Irish soil," George W. Bush was shielded from thousands of Irish protesters at the airport entrance and whisked off in an armored Cadillac to the 16th century Dromoland Castle in County Clare.

More than 34 million Americans claim Irish ancestry, and the "ould sod" has always been one of the most welcome destinations for U.S. officials; presidents Kennedy, Reagan and Clinton drew huge and admiring crowds. But the reception given President Bush signified that no place was safe from the large and growing international network of protesters whose "peace" signs mask a global movement of anti-American hatred.

The Bush trip turned Ireland into an armed camp. The turnout of 50,000 protesters in Dublin forced Irish security officials to transform the Shannon area into what the press called a "ring of steel." Six thousand officers (the "largest in the history of the island," according to the *Washington Post*) were deployed; naval gunships patrolled an estuary and armored cars searched bogs and alleys. Some of Ireland's top lawyers signed a petition suggesting the President be arrested as soon as he arrived. Clerics openly questioned his morals. The leader of the Irish Senate boycotted an embassy dinner.

What had happened? Ireland's anti-war lobby was determined to stop U.S. forces bound for Iraq from using Shannon Airport as a stopover point. (There had been over 1,000 flights carrying 55,000 troops.) They were intent on attracting the world's attention to their protests. So Mary Kelly, an Irish nurse, took a hatchet to a U.S. Navy plane at Shannon, causing $1.5 million in damages. Folk singers Christy Moore and Damien Rice recorded an anti-Bush hit single called "Lonely Soldier" and sent the recording proceeds to the anti-war movement, which organized concerts that were a build-up to the big demonstration in Dublin.

The Dublin demonstration highlighted the organizing skill of the protesters. Using bullhorns and colorful placards, rally organizers drew the media's attention to the protest itself rather than to its object, President Bush. They flooded radio phone-in shows with anti-Bush callers. And aware that one picture is still worth a thousand words, they made sure TV cameras captured the placard in an Irish hedgerow that read "No red carpet for killer Bush."

Demonstrations like these are now commonplace throughout the world. When Bush left Shannon for Ankara, Turkey, he encountered the same scene. Four policemen were injured trying to protect the U.S. president from an angry crowd of over 20,000 demonstrators who carried signs reading "USA Murderer, get out of the Middle East" and "Down with American Imperialism." Police had to teargas the crowd and blocked-off central Ankara. Bomb blasts killed four people in Istanbul. The fortress-like atmosphere around major cities prompted one Turkish commentator to write, "This visit is making our lives hell."

Explosions of anti-American temper are not new. Certainly the largest anti-American demonstration in world history occurred on February 15, 2003, when an estimated 25 million people jammed the streets of Berlin, London, Madrid, Amsterdam and Rome, Dhaka, Jakarta, Amman, Bombay, Islamabad, Hong Kong, Bangkok and most of America's largest cities. Incredibly, the protests were against an event that had yet to occur—the war in Iraq was more than a month away. Organizers mobilized twenty-five million people against a political administration that had not yet announced its intentions and timing.

Since then, the anti-war protest network has continued to mobilize opposition to the war in Iraq and to the Bush Administration. A large demonstration was held on October 25, 2003 in Washington, D.C. (Other protests were held in other U.S. and foreign cities.) With 30,000 to 50,000 protestors in the nation's capital, the turnout was less than expected. But it was reminiscent of Vietnam-era protests as the demonstrators came to Washington in 150 buses from over 140 cities, chanting and waving placards: "Bush lied, thousands died," "No blood for oil," "Bring them home now." Thousands gathered in the shadow of the Washington Monument as the Reverend Al Sharpton screamed from the podium, " Don't give Bush 87 billion dollars... don't give him 87 cents." A *New York Times* reporter noted, "The demonstration borrowed heavily from the imagery of 1960's peace protests over Vietnam, as young people in tie-dyed shirts and bandanas waved placards bearing peace signs and exhorted the White House to 'make love, not war.' "

Small wonder! Many of the organizers against the Iraq War are the same people who in 1968 disrupted the nation during the Vietnam War and helped push Lyndon Johnson from office.

The new anti-war movement has centered on an umbrella group named International ANSWER (an acronym for "Act Now to Stop War and End Racism"). However, under that new name is an old political group: ANSWER is an off-spring of Workers World, a Communist splinter party.

ANSWER and other left-wing groups are subjecting the Bush Administration's global war on terrorism, especially the war in Iraq, to some of the largest protests actions since the Vietnam War. Indeed, the current movement mobilized more demonstrations and protests in only four months—from the U.N. deadline of November 7, 2002 to the launch of Operation Iraqi Freedom on March 20, 2003—than Vietnam-era protest groups mobilized during the first six years of U.S. involvement (1961 – 1967).

ANSWER and a second group called United for Peace and Justice along with thousands of other allied satellite groups organized the massive protests on March 20, 2004 that marked the first anniversary of the war in Iraq. And while there have been no demonstrations since the President's reelection in November, they are sure to resume. Like sharks sensing blood in the water, the slightest drop in President Bush's standing in public opinion will provoke a frenzy of activism. These groups are not assuaged and they do not rest. Those who remember how the 1968 Democratic convention in Chicago sparked violent protests worry that the January 20, 2005 inauguration of the President will also begin a new era of anti-war violence.

Analysts of anti-war activism often focus on election results or overseas events to predict the scope of domestic unrest. But that fails to recognize that protests and demonstrations are a tactic. They are meant to serve a long-term political strategy. Leftist organizers have goals that are much greater than simply "ending the war." We may be at the start of another long period of civil disorder in America.

Peace Tactics

The irony of the modern "peace" movement is that it has very little to do with peace—either as a moral concept or as a political ideal. Peace is a tactical ideal for movement organizers: it serves as political leverage against U.S. policymakers, and it is an ideological response to the perceived failures of American society. The leaders of anti-war groups are modern-day Leninists. As Lenin used Russian war-weariness in 1917 to overthrow the Czar, so American street revolutionaries use reactions to the war on Al-Qaeda and Saddam Hussein as a way to foment radical political change at home.

The current peace movement is "neo-Communist," says David Horowitz, the one-time radical-turned-conservative. This is a revealing and accurate label. In fact, the movement is heir to the Communist Party of the United States of America (CPUSA), even though the party's global base—the Soviet Union—no longer exists.

A variety of CPUSA splinter groups claim the mantle of the Left even as they spin-off a dizzying series of front groups and issue-oriented action "committees." ANSWER is only the largest of these groups, which also include United for Peace and Justice, Code Pink, Not In Our Name, the Green Party and the Institute for Policy Studies. The Bush Administration's war on terror, which includes the Iraq war, has prompted all of them to form coalitions and seek allies. Their aim is a "struggle" against "oppression" and "imperialism," code words in the lexicon of revolutionary socialism. Not In Our Name (NION), a satellite of the Revolutionary Communist Party, decries the War on Terror as a Bush Administration ploy: "We will not stop until all of us are free from your bloodthirsty domination."

After the attacks of 9/11, when the enemy targeted Americans for terror and death, the need for a "peace movement" vanished. Remember the isolationist group America First? On December 11, 1941, four days after Pearl Harbor, it honorably disbanded, declaring "The time for military action is here." But the current movement does just the opposite. As this study demonstrates, many of today's anti-war organizers used to support the Soviet Union and its proxies such as the Vietcong, the Sandinistas, North Korea, Castro's Cuba and the Communist guerrillas in El Salvador. It is no exaggeration to say that the modern peace movement is composed of the ideological remnants of Communism. These groups are motivated by anti-Americanism, anti-capitalism, anti-Semitism and anti-globalization. They are enamored of socialism, world revolution and class solidarity.

The anti-war movement has a deep-seated hostility to any use of American power. The fact that groups mobilized so quickly in *anticipation* of Operation Iraqi Freedom suggests that they are not simply anti-war. Similarly, many campus activists denounced the war at the very moment when Saddam Hussein's forces appeared utterly defeated by the U.S. military (i.e., well before the Iraq insurgency). The demonstrators wanted to protest *any* U.S. military actions, including those that successfully defeated a tyrannical regime.

Student/faculty demonstrations at over 150 campuses have been the mainspring for much anti-American activism. The scene at UCLA was typical. In April 2003, less than a week after the fall of Saddam Hussein, the UCLA faculty senate approved a resolution by a margin of 180 – 7 to "condemn" the "United States invasion of Iraq." The senate also voted to "deplore the doctrine of preventive war the President has used to justify the invasion" and to "oppose the establishment of the American protectorate in Iraq."

The resolution's co-author was a veteran Marxist sociology professor named Maurice Zeitlin. He wrote one of the first pro-Castro books published in the U.S. in 1961 and was an anti-Vietnam war activist. At a 1997 UCLA symposium Zeitlin praised Cuba's Che Guevara, who once declared that the U.S. deserved to suffer through "two, three... many Vietnams." Said Zeitlin: "Che was above all a revolutionary socialist and a leader of the first socialist revolution in this hemisphere. His legacy is embodied in the fact that Cuban revolution is alive today despite the collapse of the Soviet bloc... No social justice is possible without a vision like Che's."

Professor Zeitlin is no lonely dinosaur of the left. Over 14,000 professors signed protest petitions against the Bush Administration. At Columbia a "teach-in" led by thirty faculty members featured anthropology professor Nicholas DeGenova, who declared that America should lose the war and deserved "a million Mogadishus" (the city in Somalia where 18 U.S. soldiers were killed in 1993).

Leftist publications trumpet the revival of the anti-war movement. The pages of the *Nation,* a leading organ of the ideological left since the Popular Front in the 1930s, have taken on new life. Michael T. Klare, a regular contributor and co-signer of the professors' petition, wrote "Resist War and Empire," a clarion call to oppose the war. Even as UN inspectors searched for weapons of mass destruction, Klare wrote, "The peace movement must prepare itself to conduct a long-term struggle against the Administration's imperial designs in the gulf. These plans must be exposed for what they are: a classic appropriation of political power and material goods (especially petroleum) by material force masquerading as a campaign for democracy."

In confronting the anti-war movement we need to understand that our country is at stake, not just a president or administration. The anti-war movement is motivated by its analysis of what the United States *is*, not by what the Bush Administration *does*. The movement is not dedicated to pacifism. Like the films of Michael Moore, it is a political revolution in the making. With a safe haven and base at leading U.S. universities, the movement is protected by academic discourse about "imperialism" and "globalization," watchwords for an anti-American political agenda. By design, these ideas spill over into the streets and turn ugly.

Ugly as in anti-Semitic. While up to 50,000 demonstrators marched in Washington, D.C. on Saturday, October 25, 2003, several thousand more protested in San Francisco. According to eyewitness Greg Yardley, "those stumbling onto the protest by accident might be forgiven for thinking it was really against Israel." Speakers denounced Israel and the U.S. in equal measure. Ban al-Wardi of the American-Arab Anti-Discrimination Committee declared that America and Israel were paying a heavy price for the intervention in Iraq and that Palestinians and Iraqis had a legitimate right to "resist." He observed that Israel was "ethnically cleansing" itself of Palestinians and attacked Attorney General John Ashcroft's "Israelization" of the U.S. justice system. Zulma Oliveras, a Puerto Rican separatist, trivialized the Holocaust: "We must stop the lie that only one holocaust has happened." "I want you to die for Israel," read the placard of one man in an Uncle Sam suit; on his lapel was an Israeli flag next to a swastika.

The political causes were more diverse at a June 27, 2003 demonstration in Burlingame, California organized by International ANSWER. Present on that occasion were the Arab-American Anti-Discrimination Committee, the National Organization for Women, Al-Awda (the Palestinian Right of Return Coalition), Global Exchange, Peace and Justice Center, the South Bay Mobilization, Children's Defense Fund, and Not In Our Name.

The protestors' objective was to disrupt a fundraising luncheon for President Bush. Display tables featured *Workers World, Revolutionary Worker* and *Socialist Action*—each the organ of a rival Communist organization. There were leaflets and stickers announcing "U.S. and Israel – Partners in Crime" and "Bush Lied, People Died." A flyer from the "Labor Action Committee to Free Mumia Abu-Jamal" urged action to help free the notorious inmate convicted of murdering a Philadelphia policeman. Rep. Barbara Lee, a radical who has replaced Ron Dellums as Berkeley, California's representative in Congress, was present. So was Green Party candidate Pat Gray, the 2004 opponent of Democratic Rep. Tom Lantos. (Workers World Party members distributed "Drop Lantos, Not Bombs" flyers.)

Demonstrators carried Palestinian and Cuban flags and wore Che Guevara T-shirts. Members of the group Rainforest wore T-shirts supporting the Mexican rebel group EZLN. Although ostensibly a peace protest, speakers endorsed a range of violent leftist revolutionary causes. One supported the FARC revolutionary movement against the government of Colombia; another represented the "Committee to Free the Cuban Five" (five Cuban spies arrested by the U.S.). A speaker from Global Exchange, the anti-trade group, accused the U.S. government of conspiring in the crash of the airliner that hit the Pentagon on September 11. The crowd cheered.

The leaders of International ANSWER have shown they can mobilize demonstrators worldwide with little advance notice. Modern communications technology makes it possible for ANSWER to alert its affiliates to loose thousands of demonstrators into the streets. On March 20, 2004 ANSWER organized marches across the globe against the U.S. war on terror. Working with another communist-front group, United for Peace and Justice, ANSWER sent out a bulk email just days before the planned marches praising Spain's decision to pull out of Iraq. It declared, "The people of Spain will be in the streets on March 20th. So must we."

Not surprisingly, the left-wing international press enthusiastically broadcast the news. *Xinhua* in China, Australia's *Sunday Times* and other newspapers condemned the U.S. and urged on the protesters. Australians chanted "End the occupation, troops out, [Prime Minister John] Howard out" on the same day that 10,000 demonstrators marched in Athens, 30,000 in Tokyo, and 25,000 in London. Thousands gathered outside the U.S. military base in Ramstein, Germany.

America Last

What's the difference between what may be termed legitimate forms of peace advocacy and the subterfuge of today's "peace" movement? The difference can be measured by looking closely at the organization and tactics of the groups that have staked out positions on the war on terror. Open policy debate over war and peace promotes democracy, but the advocacy of political insurrection destroys it. By this measure the "Call to Action" announced in the summer of 2004 by International ANSWER, the largest anti-war umbrella organization, is nothing less than a comprehensive attack on American democracy.

The "Call" offers a long-term ideological agenda of ways to attack the United States. It demands worldwide revolution against America's political, social and economic institutions and policies. Its proponents summon opposition wherever the American flag flies. Like an earlier Manifesto, the Call bears close reading at length:

The twin parties of the war machine are gathering this summer in Boston and New York City to anoint their candidates for the upcoming presidential election. It is urgent that the progressive movement be in the streets in Boston and New York City.

This is a critical time for all progressives and targeted communities to take a clear stand against the political framework that is championed by the Republican and Democratic parties alike.... From imprisoning the Palestinian people with an Apartheid Wall, to occupying Haiti through death-squad proxies and the deployment of U.S. troops, to turning Afghanistan and Central Asia into a U.S. sphere of influence, the U.S. government is using its military power to carry out the corporate looting of the world's natural and human resources....

As the federal government rapidly shifts funds to the already bloated Pentagon budget, a move initiated by Bush and supported by Kerry, funds available for states and cities and especially needed social programs are being slashed. Devastating cuts in housing, education, training, veterans benefits, and healthcare are imposing a new level of human suffering especially in working class and poor communities. Hardest hit are the African-American and Latino communities.

Both parties are opposed to providing benefits and legal safeguards to undocumented workers and their families. Both parties have engaged in scapegoating and targeting of immigrant communities and their legal and social rights....

The emergence of a mass global movement in the last three years has shown the depth of the outrage against the Bush Administration's global agenda, its criminal actions and its propensity to limitless violence in the pursuit of world domination, empire and Pax Americana. The whole world is threatened by the Bush regime. Not only have there been wars and occupations in Iraq and Afghanistan and the U.S. coup and occupation of Haiti, the first Black republic in the western hemisphere, but all the people of the world realize that they are in the cross-hairs. The establishment of new military bases in the former Soviet Republics in the Caspian region and the re-introduction of U.S. military forces in the Philippines indicates the dangers posed by the Bush government. The administration is committed to the overthrow of the government of Cuba and the Chavez government in Venezuela. They are committed to the overthrow of the government of Zimbabwe and the semi-colonial reconquest of Africa.... It is recklessly and rapidly building its so-called Missile Defense system which puts the U.S. on a collision course with the People's Republic of China and North Korea. The people of the Middle East recognize that the Iraq war was designed to set the stage for further threats, aggression and intervention in Syria, Lebanon, Iran and other countries in the region....

We also know that what has not stopped the Bush Administration is the Democratic Party, because that Party is an expression of the same corporate establishment and Military-Industrial complex in whose interest the Bush Administration functions.... Both parties and both conventions represent the concentration of power in the hands of corporate and banking elites, the extension of militarism and war, and the assault carried out by the corporate establishment against worker's rights, civil rights and civil liberties. It was the massive and independent mobilization of the people that won union rights in the 1930's, civil rights in the 1960's and the advance in women's and lesbian/gay/bi/trans rights. It was the people of the United States, combined with the resistance in Vietnam and around the world, which brought that criminal war in Southeast Asia to an end.

The real hope for change, not cosmetic alterations but the urgently needed profound social change in the United States, will come about from an enlarged and politically conscious mass movement of the people. This movement is in an embryonic state, its potential dynamic evolution is the real source of optimism in global politics but its potential will rapidly evaporate if it settles for the meager role of tail to the kite of the Democratic Party establishment.

Whether ANSWER and its fellow-travelers believe their indictment of the United States need not concern most Americans. But that leaders of countries in the U.N. General Assembly parrot its line and encourage foreign news media to present it as fact is of grave concern. U.S. anti-war groups are responsible for spreading and legitimating reporting and analysis of this sort. For over three years, they have broadcast falsehoods to the world media, to nongovernmental organizations (NGOs) and to the global elite.

The United States is now out-of-favor with the so-called "world community," which began to discredit the Bush Administration after it refused to endorse the Kyoto Accord on global warming and the International Criminal Court. Then in summer 2001, official delegates and NGOs attending the U.N. World Conference Against Racism in Durban, South Africa so pummeled the U.S. that Secretary of State Colin Powell instructed U.S. delegates to withdraw from the event. The offensive against America continued after the U.S. military defeated the Taliban and Saddam Hussein. The insurgency inside Iraq and President Bush's reelection only provide further excuses for the anti-war movement to continue to attack American democracy.

The ANSWER "Call" is a declaration of war on American values, and we can expect its political offensive to continue. It is interesting to note that the ANSWER statement ends with a nostalgic tribute to the "progressives" of the 1930's and the 1960's—the leftist movements that spawned the current generation of activists. Unlike too many modern Americans, anti-war activists appreciate the importance of history—even as they distort it.

Of course, opposition to war policies need not be anti-American. Chapters three and four of this study recount America's history of anti-war activity. Honorable Americans opposed the Mexican War (including Lincoln and Grant) and the war against Spain. However, their opposition was rooted in patriotism, and they warned that U.S. expansion into Latin America and the Philippines threatened the institutions of American democracy.

Peace advocacy flourished during the first four decades of the twentieth century and found favor with many prominent Americans who held a variety of political opinions. Andrew Carnegie underwrote the Carnegie Endowment for International Peace and President Woodrow Wilson campaigned for a "war to end all wars" and a League of Nations. In the 1920's an emerging Eastern Establishment of lawyers and diplomats constructed a foreign policy for three Republican presidents that proposed to cut armaments and "outlaw" war through diplomacy. Western populists such as William Jennings Bryan and William Borah opposed entangling alliances to keep the U.S. at peace. So did members of the group America First before World War II. Its supporters ranged from the socialist Norman Thomas to Charles A. Lindbergh, "the Lone Eagle." Midwestern Republicans like Senator Robert A. Taft were deeply troubled by America's new Cold War responsibilities. All opposed government policies they deemed likely to increase the risk of war. None were anti-American.

But beginning in the 1930's the radical Left captured the bullhorn for peace activism, and there it has remained for the past seventy-five years. Anti-war activism has come to represent anti-Americanism—a movement of individuals who regard the nation with open contempt. Major anti-war organizations make excuses for terrorists and express support for those who sympathize with them. Their leaders command thousands of followers who will turn out for protests en masse.

Unfortunately, democracies in wartime are at a disadvantage. American diplomacy, especially American public diplomacy, has not been as valiant as the U.S. military. Advocates of American policy and institutions are on the defensive. And violence inside Iraq has compounded U.S. tactical awkwardness, playing into the hands of anti-war groups. Americans understandably have little patience with protracted or indecisive military campaigns, and American politicians fear a political "quagmire"—when short wars turn into long and difficult military campaigns.

The military draft spurred much youthful protest during the era of the Vietnam War—but there is no draft now. That makes the current scope of anti-war/anti-Bush rallies all the more remarkable, particularly their worldwide scale. "Peace" groups today deserve a new name: America Last.

Anti-War Protest:
In and Against American History

The test of American democracy is the durability of our

political institutions and the solidarity of our political culture. That our institutions fulfill their mission during wartime and under conditions of intense domestic political attack is a rare quality, one shared by few other societies in the world. Our democracy is healthy because radicals—at least so far—are unable to disrupt it.

However, today we are in a desperate struggle against a vicious enemy, and it would be a mistake to dismiss the anti-war movement because it appears small and splintered. Small and splintered political groups have produced large and tragic consequences. Every administration confronts abundant criticism and dissent. But the current peace *movement* is a unique political subculture organized to orchestrate political protest. Its record is varied and important, full of both dismal setbacks and spectacular gains that have affected U.S. national security for better and worse. We need to know more about it.

I want to put the current movement in perspective. I argue that it is not a spontaneous popular or grassroots opposition to America's counterattack on terror. Instead, the movement is the product of several generations of radical opposition to America's political and social order. Peace activism is not an isolated, unique or contemporary phenomenon. Current anti-war protest groups have long histories; some can be traced back to the radical protest groups that opposed the Vietnam War. Others go even further back to Communist organizations of the 1950's and 1930's. Under the corrosive influence of Marxist ideology, "peace" activism is another name for the advocacy of violence and revolution.

This book has an unusual organization. The first two chapters discuss the current anti-war movement. The next three are a historical review of the history of anti-war activism in America. My discussion there begins with the movement for "Manifest Destiny" in the mid-nineteenth century. But it might just as well begin with the Puritans, who in the seventeenth century must have been the most radical political sect on earth.

The writer Louis Menand links modern war protest to the Puritans when he observes of the "Woodstock generation" of 1969: "The counterculture wasn't hedonistic; it was puritanical. It was, in fact, virtually Hebraic; the parents were worshiping false gods, and the students who tore up (or dropped out of) the

13

university in an apparent frenzy of self-destructiveness ... were, in effect, smashing the golden calf." Similarly, the political scientist Michael Walzer finds a common psychological dynamic in the Puritans, the Jacobins, the Bolsheviks and the New Left. Each movement produced the "soldier-saint": "The saint is a soldier whose battles are fought out in the self before they are fought out in society. Revolution follows from Puritan sainthood—that is, from the triumph over Satanic lusts ... It is the acting out of a new identity."

The scholar Adam Garfinkle also finds the roots of anti-war protest in the zealotry of America's Puritan "counterculture." In *Telltale Hearts,* his history of the anti-Vietnam War movement, Garfinkle writes, "While the antiwar movement appears to have come before the counterculture, in a more fundamental sense, the counterculture was the source of it all." The Puritan counter-culture with its profound dissatisfaction with all things of this earth, he observes, pre-dated the American Revolution by more than a century.

That brings up a second reason for this book. I want to explain how American anti-war protest has changed. Since 1776 protest and revolution have been critical parts of the American heritage. As I point out in chapters three and four, anti-war activism was part of the progressive reform tradition at the start of the twentieth century. Conservatives also have been staunch opponents of war policies. We should not be blinded by the current image of anti-war activists as rowdy street protesters. Throughout our history activists have included elders of the church, pillars of the establishment and millionaire businessmen. These figures have had far more impact on our history and society than several generations of Berkeley sophomores.

Woodrow Wilson is arguably the preeminent modern anti-war radical. After all, he fought the Great War (World War I) as a "war to end all wars." This must be counted one of the great acts of political dissent. Wilson's ghost still haunts American foreign policy—lest we forget George H.W. Bush, who proclaimed a "new world order" even as he issued a disclaimer on the "vision thing." The first President Bush only reflected the same yearning for a higher political order that has challenged and frustrated anti-war agitators for centuries. We need to remember that not all protest

14

movements are ugly and negative; many begin with a vaunted and utopian vision of what should be.

Finally, this book intends to remind readers that anti-war sentiments are not the same as anti-war political activism. Peace advocates can be high-minded or fanatical, reformist or revolutionary, but it takes protracted conflict before advocacy becomes political activism. Unpopular and destabilizing wars fuel radical activism better than anything else.

The case studies presented in chapter three illustrate the political costs of small wars. A conventional victory turns into frustrating counter-insurgency: here is the ideal breeding ground for anti-war political protest. The case studies demonstrate that the insurgency in Iraq is far from unique in our history.

Chapter 1

HOMEFRONT:
THE WAR AGAINST THE WAR ON TERROR

In 1963 Todd Gitlin helped found the anti-war group Students for a Democratic Society (SDS). He became perhaps the country's most articulate New Left theoretician during the Vietnam War era and is today a Columbia University sociology professor. Gitlin acknowledges that today's peace movement is inspired by the opponents of the Vietnam war (and thus, in a way, by himself), but he has distanced himself from the new movement, claiming that it lacks "vitality" and is not sufficiently "inventive." This elder statesman of protest blames Ralph Nader and the Greens for the election of George W. Bush in 2000, and he is particularly scornful of ANSWER's role in organizing protests against the war in Iraq. ANSWER's tactics and rhetoric, he feels, are more akin to the "fanaticism" of the radical Weatherman faction of SDS, who talked "a sort of abstract language which doesn't make sense to anyone not standing in their immediate circle."

Remarkably, Gitlin sees the Republicans, who were able to elect both Ronald Reagan and George W. Bush twice, as the model for efficient political organization. "Everybody on the left should go listen to the Republicans," he scolded recently, "and try to figure out what makes them tick." Shortly after 9/11, Gitlin advised the nascent antiwar movement to "re-examine their doctrines if they hope to influence events." The repertoire of the new groups, he felt, was overly-influenced by the Vietnam experience: "Generals, it is said, are always fighting the last war. ... The same is true of the anti-war movement. The movement is a child of the Vietnam era and has viewed every subsequent conflict through that prism."

While it may be easy to second-guess Gitlin's new-found maturity, his point is well-taken. Political movements may suffer major tactical reverses but they must adjust over the long term. Every successful political movement thinks strategically, adapting circumstance to circumstance, generation to generation. Today's battle is against international terrorism. But there are some groups making war on the war on terror, and they are directly related to the anti-Vietnam War movement of not-so-long-ago. Twenty-six years, less than a generation, separate the end of the Vietnam War in 1975 and September 11, 2001. It's not only possible that the radical activists who undermined U.S. policies and resolve back then might be active now—it's a fact.

From 1975 to 2001 the anti-war movement was quiescent because there were few U.S. wars to protest. The U.S. military interventions in Lebanon, Grenada and Panama ended too quickly for protesters to launch major anti-war demonstrations. And NATO's bombing of Belgrade, deemed "humanitarian" by many liberals, generated little dissent. Of course, leftist activists do not need an actual war to organize a protest movement. The root cause of war for them is always the same—it's "the system" and its component parts: American "racism," "sexism" and "capitalism."

In the 1980's and 1990's would-be anti-war protestors turned to other causes and other victims. For a time they focused on "globalization," which is supposed to mean U.S. exploitation of the world's environment, economic development, minority rights and civil liberties. The United Nations held enormous conferences in Cairo on population control (1994); Beijing on feminism (1995); Rio (1993) and Kyoto (1997) on environmentalism and global warming; and Durban, South Africa on racism (2001). These gatherings attracted thousands of participants from nongovernmental groups (NGOs), who, absent a major war, attempted to make these issues the focus of international political activism.

Of course, the Gulf War was a major exception; it generated considerable protest before the war was stopped short. Former U.S. Attorney General Ramsey Clark led the National Coalition

18

to Stop U.S. Intervention in the Middle East, which held rallies in early 1991. Holdover groups from the Vietnam era served as coalition partners, including Vietnam Veterans Against the War, the Revolutionary Communist Party, Progressive Labor Party, War Resisters League, American Friends Service Committee, SANE, Women Strike for Peace, and the Women's International League for Peace and Freedom. Mainline churches, too, were outspoken against the Gulf War, as were a host of newer advocacy groups: Greenpeace, Physicians for Social Responsibility, ACT-UP, Hands Off Cuba, and the Palestine Human Rights Committee.

However, the first Bush Administration avoided major anti-war conflict at home by declaring victory abroad. It left Saddam Hussein in power and never challenged the Vietnam "syndrome" that has left U.S. domestic politics and foreign policy hamstrung for decades. As historian Paul Boyer observed, "With the benefit of hindsight, what strikes one is not how rapidly an antiwar movement surfaced, but how quickly it was buried in a blizzard of flags, yellow ribbons, media images of high-tech weaponry, and 'welcome home' parades heavy with military hardware."

The Anti-War Movement Reborn

The current anti-war movement is heir to the Vietnam generation. In the 1960's well-organized and well-financed revolutionary groups gained control of the "peace movement." The shrill voices of revolutionary Marxist agitators and dreamy socialist visionaries dominated the protest movement (and overwhelmed the more sober objections of Christian theologians such as Reinhold Niebuhr and writers of the so-called realist school of foreign policy such as Hans Morgenthau and George Kennan).

It's happening all over again. The language of today's peace movement is almost exclusively negative and anti-American. All aspects of our country's culture, politics and economics come under attack. Moreover, the movement is united under a revolutionary banner—only it's not the American Revolution.

Marx, Trotsky, Lenin, Stalin, Mao and Castro are its forebears. Anyone reading the public speeches and writings of spokesmen for the major anti-war groups and perusing dozens of their websites will encounter hatred of America coupled with praise for Ho Chi Minh, Slobodan Milosevic, Kim Il-sung and his son Kim Jong-il—and Saddam Hussein.

These common denominators describe the peace movement today. The names of the major groups—ANSWER, Not in Our Name, United for Peace and Justice, Code Pink—are meant to deceive. Under their banners march revolutionary cadres and professional agitators.

Comprised of various Communist party factions, these groups know how to organize protest demonstrations in the name of peace. They are classic "front" groups— umbrella organizations whose purpose is to attract well-meaning innocents to support the "party line." Front groups have been the stock-in-trade of the Comintern and the worldwide Communist movement since the 1920's, when Soviet agents adopted the practice of disguising their agendas behind attractive liberal marquees.

Stalinist organizations perfected the tactic. By recruiting anyone—student, professor or Hollywood screenwriter—who believed in the cause of the moment ("peace," "human rights," "democracy"), they secured apologists for the Gulag, the Red Terror and the Red Army. During the Cold War, front groups proliferated behind the Soviet Union's "Peace Offensive." In 1951 the much-maligned House Committee on Un-American Activities described the peace offensive this way:

The most dangerous hoax ever devised by the international Communist conspiracy is the current world-wide "peace" offensive. It has received the official endorsement of the Supreme Soviet of the U.S.S.R. The Information Bureau of the Communist and Workers Parties (Cominform), ... has given this campaign top priority. It has been designated as the major effort of every Communist Party on the face of the globe, including the Communist Party of the United States. ...

The Communist "peace" movement assumes different forms at various times and places. This is calculated to disguise its Communist origin and to evade legal prosecution. Thus, we find the movement appearing as the World Congress of Intellectuals, The International Committee of Intellectuals in Defense of Peace, The World Peace

Congress or the World Congress of Partisans of Peace and American Continental Congress for Peace, all with identical slogans and propaganda, and espoused by the same group with slight variation.

Workers World Party

The largest and most prominent of the anti-war front groups today is ANSWER, which organized the massive worldwide marches of March 20, 2004. It made its first organized appearance in 2001. But ANSWER is no spontaneous grassroots civic group; it is a direct off-shoot of the Workers World Party (WWP), which was organized long ago, in 1959.

WWP was formed when five members of the Socialist Workers Party, itself a Trotskyite splinter group, left the party over differences they considered fundamental. The five protested the "rightist" slant of the Socialist Workers, according to their statement issued in the first edition of their newspaper, *Workers World,* which is still in publication:

We were the proletariat left wing of the Socialist Workers Party. We have now split with that party, which has gone further and further to the right in recent years, so that we can openly fight for orthodox Trotskyism, which is the authentic Marxism-Leninism of today.

Under long-time leader Sam Marcy (1911-1998) WWP supported Soviet suppression of the Hungarian Revolution, opposed Mikhail Gorbachev, and sided with the enemies of Boris Yeltsin ("the most outspoken reactionary leader of the bourgeois counterrevolution"). WWP gained adherents and followers through evasive strategic and tactical devises and organizational deceptions. The creation of ANSWER is but the latest in a series of ruses that stretch back decades.

WWP variously set up or absorbed other organizations that acted as its front groups. They had names like the Center for United Labor Action, Youth Against War and Fascism, Prisoners Solidarity Committee, Women United for Action, the American Servicemen's Union and the Committee to Support Middle East Liberation. The groups could merge or break apart, spinning off new groups and invent new titles as needed. This tactical elasticity gave WWP great flexibility in pursuing its ongoing "struggle." A 1974 House Committee on Internal Security report observed that the tactic of "cover organization names" was useful to WWP, allowing it "to pretend broader support for its actions than actually exists." The Report elaborated on the front tactics employed by WWP then, and still currently in use:

An example of how the Workers World Party uses a variety of names to pretend broader support for its actions ... was shown by an article in the Delaware State News for March 22, 1971. According to this account, an anti-Vietnam War rally was held in Wilmington, Del., under the sponsorship of Youth Against War and Fascism. Only one of the speakers ... was identified in the article as a member of YAWF; the other speakers were listed as "Andy Stapp, chairman of the American Serviceman's Union; David Axel, union organizer for drug and hospital workers; [and] Sharon Chin of the Free Angela Davis Committee." Despite the fact that they hid behind other organizational names, however, all three are in fact members of the Workers World Party and/or YAWF.

Amazingly, many of the current leaders of the WWP/ANSWER anti-war coalition can trace their roots back to the creation of the party. Their goals and rhetoric have remained remarkably consistent over time, which is a tribute to their long-term commitment. For instance, Deirdre Griswold (born 1936), the party's 1980 presidential candidate, is an ANSWER leader and the editor of *Workers World* newspaper (circulation: 6,000). Griswold succeeded her father, Vincent Copeland, as the newspaper's editor. He was a co-founder of WWP and in the late 1960's was a leader of the National Mobilization Committee to End the War in Vietnam. The MOBE, as it was called, organized the 1968 March on Washington that drew 500,000 protesters and helped topple Lyndon Johnson. The party supported the Viet Cong and North Vietnam, urging activists in an April 8, 1972 letter to demonstrate in support of a Viet Cong offensive in South Vietnam.

On May 2, 1975, the *Workers World* headline read, "Vietnam Belongs to the Workers!" Today, under Griswold's direction, it lauds Slobodan Milosevic and Saddam Hussein as victims of American oppression.

WWP's Trotskyite ideology has changed little over the years:

Capitalism is the problem; immediate world revolution is the solution. Even in the current dark times for WWP socialists, Cuba and North Korea are beacons of hope. In the early 1970's WWP helped organize trips to both countries through front groups like the American Servicemen's Union and the Venceremos Brigade.

The 1974 House committee report identified another WWP group, the Committee To Support Middle East Liberation (CSMEL), as a "front that operates in support of Arab terrorists in the Middle East." The House committee quoted from a CSMEL statement explaining why terror tactics were "just" and "progressive":

The only way a change of thinking could come about is precisely if the Arabs could inflict a series of heavy military defeats on Israel. World War I was a war waged by the falling out of imperialists through economic rivalries for control of imperialistic exploitation of the globe, whereas the Israeli-Arab conflict and especially the struggle of the Palestinian Liberation Organization is in essence a war of national liberation, which by definition is just, progressive and anti-imperialist.

Workers World even expressed solidarity with the terrorists who attacked the Munich Olympics in 1972, killing eleven Israeli athletes and a German policeman:

It is U.S. imperialism which is responsible for the bloodshed at Munich, in the Middle East, in Indochina, and the world over. And it is the imperialists who are the real terrorists, the real menace to humanity, who terrorize workers and oppressed people daily. And until their terror is wiped out, the killing and human misery they cause will never cease.

Now consider the most recent WWP demonstrations. The ties between WWP, the peace movement, and socialist dictators remain intact. At protest rallies in 2003 and 2004, WWP continued to link the anti-war cause to the defense of North Korea. For instance, Yoomi Chong of the Korea Truth Commission (KTC) was a featured speaker at a January 18, 2003 protest march. KTC is tied to another WWP front group, the International Action Center, which created ANSWER.

In a show of support for North Korea, the KTC has sent eight delegations to Pyongyang, all of them organized by Ramsey Clark. Full of praise for the longest-running Communist dictatorshop on earth, they are reminiscent of the infamous pilgrimages fellow travelers made to Stalin's Soviet Union during the 1920's and 30's. The North Korean capital, Pyongyang, is portrayed as a "Potemkin village" in the following report from the eighth KTC delegation:

To the visitor, Pyongyang leaves the impression of a clean, modern world capital. It is a city of two million people with an efficient public transportation system, wide, tree-lined streets, and all the cultural amenities, hospitals, schools, parks and sports facilities that one would expect to find in a large metropolis. Industry has been located on the perimeter of the city to avoid the problem of pollution as much as possible ... the people of Pyongyang present themselves as cultured and purposeful. There is no sign of vagrancy or homelessness. Instead of billboards with product advertising, the streets are adorned with posters, banners and inscriptions exhorting citizens to work together to build a powerful nation.

Deirdre Griswold traveled to North Korea in April 2002 to celebrate the 90th anniversary of the birth of Kim Il-sung. There she denounced the "notorious antiterrorist war" of the Bush Administration and called for "the Korean peninsula [to] be reunified without fail under the wise leadership of the respected leader Kim Jong-il..." Brian Becker, a party leader and vice-chairman of another WWP front, the Committee of the International Liaison for Unification and Peace in Korea (CILRECO), visited Pyongyang in March 2002 with a similar message. He accused the United States of a genocidal war on Korean civilians. The International Action Center then set up a Korean War Crimes Tribunal in New York. Currently, Becker is the "national coordinator" for the ANSWER Coalition.

Recently, WWP held a series of "war crimes trials" of the U.S. in Mexico, Japan, India, Denmark and Belgium. Subsequent trials are scheduled for 2005, beginning in March in Istanbul, Turkey. As reported in *Workers World* (May 20, 2004), the trial "verdicts" have convicted the U.S. of human rights violations against Iraqi civilians and violation of the Geneva Convention, and earned it the admonition "that the occupation of Palestine, Afghanistan and all other colonized areas are illegal and should be brought to an end immediately."

Another WWP front, Support Network for an Armed Forces Union (SNAFU), urges military disobedience and resistance: "Sisters and Brothers in the Armed Forces: Resist! Organize! Refuse to participate in war crimes. Join us in taking action to stop the war." An anti-draft warning in *Workers World* (June 17, 2004) threatens that SNAFU will organize nationwide street demonstrations: "We've had the opportunity to talk with several members of the military families today... The movement against the war inside this community is growing daily. SNAFU is reaching out to provide support to resisters inside the military. We're also circulating a 'no draft' petition as part of our new No Draft, No Way campaign."

A.N.S.W.E.R. (Act Now To Stop War and End Racism) and International Action Center (IAC)

The most notable of the WWP front groups is International ANSWER, the most prominent group mobilizing opposition to the war on terror to emerge since September 11. More specifically, it is the largest of the front groups that seeks every occasion to campaign against the U.S.

The head of the ANSWER steering committee is Ramsey Clark, former U.S. Attorney General during the Johnson Administration. He also heads the International Action Center (IAC), yet another front group for the Workers World Party and ANSWER. Observers say Clark fell under the influence of the WWP in the early 1990's.

Besides IAC, the other members of the ANSWER steering committee include the Korea Truth Commission and the pro-Castro Pastors for Peace, the Muslim Student Association and the Free Palestine Alliance. They provide logistical, financial and ideological support for America's enemies in the terrorist network, including Hamas. (see Appendix for an extensive list of ANSWER membership.)

ANSWER's political agenda is anti-Semitic as well as anti-American. "Chosen People: It's Payback Time" read the placards of marchers at a Free Palestine Rally sponsored by ANSWER in April 2002. Other ANSWER-supported rallies have turned away Jewish speakers and encouraged demonstrations against Israel. Ramsey Clark even provided legal counsel for anti-Israel activists, including PLO leaders. In 1987 he defended Nazi concentration camp guard Karl Linnas when the federal government attempted to deport him. Clark lost that case, complaining about the need to prosecute Nazis "forty years after some god-awful crime they're alleged to have committed."

Clark has a long record of service as a spokesman for the nation's largest anti-war and anti-Bush activist group. He has condemned the "war crimes" of U.S. presidents back to Harry Truman (who appointed his father, Tom Clark, attorney general in 1945 and to the U.S. Supreme Court in 1949). In 2001 Clark attempted to represent Slobodan Miloslevic in his war crimes trial at the World Court in the Hague. He also volunteered to represent Saddam Hussein.

In an open letter to U.N. Secretary General Kofi Annan (January 29, 2004), Clark outlined how he and ANSWER judged the U.S. war effort in Afghanistan and Iraq:

The claim that either Afghanistan or Iraq declared war on the U.S. is absurd. The U.S. chose to attack both nations, from one end to the other, violating their sovereignty and changing their 'regimes,' summarily executing thousands of men, women and children in the process. At least 40, 000 defenseless people in Iraq have been killed by U.S. violence since the latest aggression began in earnest in March 2003... The U.S. is guilty of pure aggression, arbitrary repression and false portrayal of the nature and purpose of its violence... The United Nations must recognize and declare the U.S. attack and occupation of Iraq to be the war of aggression it is.

ANSWER and Clark want President Bush impeached and prosecuted for war crimes: "There must be strict accountability by U.S. leaders and others for crimes they have committed against Iraq and Afghanistan and compensation by the U.S. government for the damage its aggression has inflicted."

Clark's group, the International Action Center (IAC), received $62,000 in 2002 from the People's Rights Fund, a 501(c)(3) public charity, according to IRS records available at www.guidestar.org. The Fund claimed 2002 revenues of $447,045 and assets of $61,458. Its president is Kathleen Durkin; its attorney is William Sacks. Interestingly, Clark's IAC, the People's Rights Fund, and the ANSWER coalition all share the same New York City address: 39 W. 14th Street.

IAC also received almost $100,000 from the Progressive Unity Fund, a 501(c)(3) with 2002 revenues of $184,415 and assets of $37,237. Its officers (President Brenda Sandburg, vice president Rosa Penate and secretary-treasurer Keith Pavlik) list their address at 167 Anderson Street in San Francisco.

Besides Clark, other prominent ANSWER members in the coalition include the Green Party USA, New Communist Party of the Netherlands, The International Family and Friends of Mumia Abu-Jamal, the National Lawyers Guild and the president of the World Union of Freethinkers. This apparent diversity is deceptive; all get at least partial funding from the same sources like the Peoples Rights Fund (PRF).

The slogans and signs at ANSWER rallies—"No Blood For Oil," "U.S. Out of the Middle East," No Justice, No Peace," and, most disingenuously of all, "Peace is Patriotic"—are its stock-in-trade. The failed Democratic presidential candidate Dennis Kucinich even unveiled his proposal for a "Department of Peace" at an ANSWER rally. But the goals of the organizations that work with ANSWER have little to do with peace and much to do with ideology.

For instance, Ray LaForest of the Haiti Support Network (HSN) opened a March 20, 2004 rally in New York with an oblique reference to peace, "I thank you for bringing your bodies to defend peace." But he immediately got to the point: "I'm here to stand with the Palestinian people, and to condemn the occupation of Iraq." The Haiti Support Network website claims "to raise material and political support for the National Popular Assembly (APN) in Haiti." But that's code for attacking U.S. policies, which APN, a leftist party, considers threatening. HSN is less an advocacy group for Haiti than it is a front for other leftist causes that want support from something that purports to represent Haitians. HSN's website is full of references to "Justice for Mumia Abu-Jamal," the convicted police killer, and pleas to end American oppressive policies. One HSN page even endorses an international conference in memory of Rosa Luxemburg, a World War I era German Communist!

"Open letters" are another time-honored tactic of activists to draw attention to their cause. In 2004 they were a clarion call to remove George Bush from office. ANSWER issued one on March 29, 2004 signed by 244 Arab and Muslim NGOs to unify the globe against the Bush Administration:

In the United States, we Arab-Americans and Muslims have been maliciously targeted, stripped of our fights, and positioned outside the constitutional framework of this country. A new COINTELPRO has been unleashed against our homes and living rooms, as our fathers, mothers, sons and daughters are plucked away and thrown into unknown prison cells. Thus, in a continuum of history, we stand with African Americans, Japanese Americans, Latinos, Native Americans, and all others in the painful struggle for justice. From them all, we take our cue for they are our predecessors and our partners in this long march.

United for Peace and Justice (UPJ)

The second largest anti-war umbrella group to emerge since 9/11 is United for Peace and Justice (UPJ). UPJ was in charge of planning the massive August 29, 2004 demonstration in New York City on the eve of the Republican National Convention. Like ANSWER, it claims to be a response to the events of 9/11. But it's also an old Soviet-style "agitprop" front group directed by a veteran Communist activist.

UPJ was created in October 2002 at a gathering of representatives of fifty diverse organizations (e.g. the Institute for Policy Studies, a left-wing think-tank, and the American Friends Service Committee, a Quaker group) who met in the offices of People for the American Way. UPJ claims responsibility for organizing hundreds of national and global protests, including the two largest in the United States on February 15, 2003 and March 22, 2003. It commands over 800 local and national groups in the United States, with worldwide affiliates on every continent.

To understand UPJ it's important to consider the pedigree of its chief operative, Leslie Cagan, a career political organizer. The *New York Times* has called her "one of the grandes dames of the country's progressive movement," a woman whose "organizational skills are prodigious." Indeed, Cagan has been active in New York City politics: She was a field director for the successful 1989 mayoral campaign of David Dinkins.

But the *Times* neglected to mention Cagan's long-standing ties to the Communist movement. Like so many peace movement leaders, Cagan is an apologist for Fidel Castro. She was a member of the Venceremos Brigade, which for thirty-five years has organized trips sending 8000 pro-Castro supporters to Cuba in violation of the U.S. travel ban. During her seven years as director of the Cuba Information Project, she led demonstrations demanding that the U.S. end its economic embargo. "In the winter of 1969-70," Cagan has recalled,

"I spent over two months with the First Venceremos Brigade in Cuba. Just ten years into their revolution, the Cubans had taken control of their history... While we were in Cuba, Fred Hampton and other Chicago Black Panthers were murdered. It was a shocking reminder of the brutality and power of the US government, and there we were in Cuba, a whole nation under attack from the US. As Brigadistas we were taking a risk traveling in defiance of Washington's travel ban, but we knew the risk was small compared to what Cubans and so many others around the world faced every day."

Cagan helped coordinate protest activities against the 1991 Gulf War through a front called the National Campaign for Peace in the Middle East. That was also the year when the Communist Party of the United States (CPUSA) broke into two factions over the politically correct attitude to take towards the collapse of the Soviet Union. Cagan and activist Angela Davis (who was once on the FBI's "Most Wanted" list) founded a revolutionary splinter group, the Committees of Correspondence for Democracy and Socialism (COC). It supported Mikhail Gorbachev against those who led the coup against him. Leaders of COC included writer Noam Chomsky and folksinger Pete Seeger. Cagan remains a COC "co-chairperson." Others with this title are Mark Solomon of the U.S. Peace Council and Charlene Mitchell, the 1968 Communist Party candidate for President.

Interestingly, there has been no love lost between ANSWER and UPJ. ANSWER functionary Sarah Sloan sneers that UPJ's differences with the U.S. government are merely "tactical," because the group's "leadership strives to find a political path that dovetails with the Democratic party." Assessing the August 31, 2004 UPJ mass protest against the Republican National Convention, Sloan concludes that Cagan supinely accommodated Democrat desires for a "tame, diffuse demonstration" that would not provoke a backlash against Kerry (*Socialism & Liberation*, October 2004).

Cagan, more cunning, applauds ANSWER for its protest actions while espousing a big tent philosophy that seeks to attract more mainstream organizations and ordinary citizens. She knows that building a "fifth column" coalition is as much a part of Leninist and Castro-style revolutionary tactics as inspiring left-wing shock troops.

Not In Our Name (NION)

The third major anti-war group is Not In Our Name (NION). Created in March 2002, NION has published newspaper ads around the world to "bring the boys home." It grew out of a "Statement of Conscience" that attracted the signatures of Noam Chomsky, historian Howard Zinn, peace activist Michael Parenti, feminists Gloria Steinem and Barbara Kingsolver, novelist Kurt Vonnegut, and Hollywood celebrity-militants Danny Glover, Tyne Daly, Jane Fonda, Oliver Stone, Marisa Tomei, Martin Sheen and Ed Harris. NION also co-sponsored a February 20, 2004 "National Day of Solidarity with Muslim, Arab and South Asian Immigrants."

NION is no less radical than ANSWER and UPJ. However, it has a different Communist mentor. ANSWER draws its organization from pro-North Korea fanatics at the Workers World Party, organized in 1959. Leslie Cagan at United for Peace and Justice looks to Fidel Castro and the Venceremos Brigades of 1969. NION's administrative cadre comes from yet another U.S. Communist splinter group, the Revolutionary Communist Party (RCP), which draws its inspiration from Communist China and Mao Tse-tung.

NION's co-directors are C. Clark Kissinger and Mary

Greenberg. Kissinger worked with the Black Panther Party in the 1960s; he founded the U.S.-China People's Friendship Association in 1971; and he supported the Iranian revolution in 1979. Kissinger's biographical statements note that he was National Secretary of Students for a Democratic Society (SDS) and organized the first March on Washington against the Vietnam War in 1965. The statement does not mention that he resigned from the U.S.-China Friendship Association after the death of Mao Tse-Tung to protest China's repudiation of the decade-long Great Proletarian Cultural Revolution, which ended in 1976 after causing the deaths of an estimated ten to 30 million people.

While pursuing his own extremist political agenda, Kissinger rounds up celebrities to oppose the war, exploiting what Lenin called the "useful idiots." Of NION's "Statement of Conscience" he has said: "We wanted people to sign the statement without having their names used to endorse other actions."

NION has allied itself with leftist and Muslim groups such as Women's International League for Peace and Freedom (WILPF), the War Resisters League (WRL), the American Muslim Council (AMC), and the Council for Palestinian Restitution and Reparation (CPRR). NION organizers include such leaders as Molly Klopot of WILPF and attorney Abdeen Jabara, a former executive director of the American-Arab Anti-Discrimination Committee, board member of the Center for Constitutional Rights, and supporter of the Indict [Ariel] Sharon Now Campaign.

NION, WILPF and the WRL share a building at 339 Lafayette Street in New York City that is owned by the A.J. Muste Memorial Institute. It has been called the "Peace Pentagon." Muste (1885-1967) was part Marxist-Leninist, part Christian pacifist, a New Left mentor and visitor to Hanoi during the Vietnam War era. The Muste Institute (2002 revenue: $478,000), which collaborates with NION and others in the peace movement, provides grants to such groups such as WILPF ($15,005 in 2002), the War Resisters League ($72,613 in 2002), Nicaragua Solidarity Network ($1,368 in 2002), International Peace Bureau in Geneva, Switzerland ($38,950 in 2002), International Fellowship of Reconciliation, and the Coalition for Human Rights of Immigrants ($3,446 in 2002).

Since May 2003 NION has employed a uniquely devious tactic dubbed "GI Special, Occupation News." The NION website daily records alleged conversations with disaffected American soldiers, who are quoted as voicing unpatriotic and radical sentiments. Typical of this daily fare is the following item, GI Special # 147 from January 1, 2004:

> Headline: Marine Says Iraq War
> "A Waste of Time, And, Most of All, Lives."

Text (selected): "I am a Marine Corps Reservist from New York. I go to college in Maryland and had to drop out of school when my unit was activated this January. I was in country from February to August. I just thought that you should know that during the deployment my unit had basically NO mission, as much as they are in denial of this.... I just thought the American taxpayers might like to know where their money is going. I wasn't too sure about this war from the beginning and now I'm certain it's a waste of time, money, and most of all, lives. ...I'm one Reservist who wouldn't re-enlist if they gave me a billion dollars." (Anonymous, 26 Nov. 2003)

NION's tangled relationship to other groups is both obscure and revealing. Donors to NION are asked to make their checks payable to "NION/IFCO" with the explanation that the "Interreligious Foundation for Community Organization (IFCO)... is our fiscal sponsor." That probably means that NION uses tax deductible contributions received by IFCO, which is a 501(c)(3) public charity registered with the IRS. The *New York Post* reports that IFCO's IRS records show that in 2000 it received $1,119,564 in contributions. A NION report declared more than $400,000 received in one year alone.

Contributions to NION/IFCO are mailed to the Women's International League for Peace and Freedom (WILPF) at the "Peace Pentagon" building that WILPF and the War Resisters League share with NION. (WILPF's Molly Klopot is a NION organizer, and WILPF executive director Marilyn Clement is IFCO's treasurer. Clement also serves on the board of the Center for Constitutional Rights.)

Founded in 1967 by leftwing church leaders, IFCO has a long pro-Castro history. IFCO executive director Lucius Walker, treasurer Marilyn Clement and grants administrator Ellen Bernstein have been pro-Castro all their lives. During a 2000 trip to Havana, for example, Walker proclaimed, "Long live the creative example of the Cuban Revolution! Long live the wisdom and heartfelt concern for the poor of the world by Fidel Castro!" Clement is co-organizer of WILPF's Sister-to-Sister Cuba project. Bernstein says Cuba is the "paradigm of democracy."

Like ANSWER, NION-IFCO defends radical Islam. IFCO is on the ANSWER Steering Committee and Lucius Walker has accompanied ANSWER's Ramsey Clark on trips to Iraq. Marilyn Clement organized Palestinians at a WILPF "solidarity" conference in May 2002, and Ellen Bernstein is a member of the American Muslim Council's campaign against the use of secret evidence. IFCO also is a fiscal sponsor of the National Coalition to Protect Political Freedom, whose co-founder is Sami Al-Arian, the University of South Florida professor indicted on terrorism charges in 2003.

The intimacy between NION and Muslim terrorist organizations is scarcely concealed. For instance, NION invited both Sami Al-Arian and radical attorney Lynne Stewart to address its October 6, 2002 rally in New York. Stewart has since been indicted for conspiring to assist terrorists. She is alleged to have carried messages from her client, Omar Abdul Rahman, the blind sheik who carried out the first World Trade Center bombing in 1993. NION leaders also cooperate with a well-funded IFCO project called the Coalition Against the "Counter Terror" Act (i.e. the USA Patriot Act).

NION leader C. Clark Kissinger aims to build what he calls "a real communist party in the U.S." Kissinger's group, the Revolutionary Communist Party (RCP) and its affiliate, the Revolutionary International Movement (RIM), are Marxist groups that promote the Leninist concept that a covert revolutionary "vanguard" must instruct party "cells" about strategic political decisions. According to the U.S. State Department, the Revolutionary International Movement (RIM) provides financial and political support to both the Communist Party of Peru (Shining Path/Sender Luminoso) and the Kurdish Workers Party (PKK). The State Department says the Communist Party of Turkey, the Union of Iranian Communists (Sarbedaran) and the Nepal Communist Party are also aligned with RIM.

A RIM publication, *A World To Win,* has declared support for the Palestinian intifada. The February 28, 2002 edition states "the Revolutionary Internationalist Movement once again reaffirms its unwavering support... and calls on all revolutionary and progressive people to step up their actions on (the Palestinians') behalf." Another issue advises Palestinians to "link up with... the parties and organizations that make up the Revolutionary Internationalist Movement. With the weapon of Marxism-Leninism-Maoism and its military strategy, people's war, the Palestinian people's fight will surely become... more integral part of the world revolution, hastening the day when imperialism, Zionism... meet their doom."

These terrorist organizations use the international drug trade to support themselves. Testifying (December 13, 2000) before a House Judiciary subcommittee on crime, counter-terrorism expert Frank Cilluffo explained that the Kurdistan Workers Party (PKK) "is heavily involved in the European drug trade, especially in Germany and France. French law enforcement estimates that the PKK smuggles 80 percent of the heroin in Paris." Cilluffo subsequently became a special assistant to President Bush in the White House office of Homeland Security.

Cilluffo also revealed that the Nepal Communist Party, "...turned to drug trafficking for funding. Nepal serves as a hub for hashish trafficking in Asia." The CIA's *World Factbook* lists Nepal as a major source for heroin from Southeast Asia to the West. The online South Asia Terrorism Portal (www.satp.org) wrote of the Nepal Communist Party: "The Maoists (Nepal) draw inspiration from the 'Revolutionary International Movement, among whose affiliates is the American Revolutionary Communist Party that provides them their ideological sustenance." Observers note the similarities in policies and tactics of Nepalese Maoists to Peru's Shining Path. Maoist violence has already cost Nepal several hundred lives and destruction of property worth millions of rupees. Over 5,000 people have been killed in Nepal since 1996, the year the insurgency began.

The Green Party and Code Pink

The peace movement can take on varying shades and hues to

camouflage itself. That's plainly the case for two groups—the Green Party and Code Pink—that have tinted their names to hide their objectives.

The "Greens" were founded in Germany in 1984 and transplanted to American soil in the 1990's. They have not achieved in America the degree of power they wield in Europe, but Greens are a threat to U.S. national security, not least because they have organized themselves as a legitimate political party. Now the largest independent, or "third," party in the U.S., having won three percent of the 2000 presidential vote with Ralph Nader as their candidate, the Greens cost the Democrats control of the White House. By 2002 they held 170 state and local offices.

A committed Marxist program hides behind the party's environmental front. The party has joined ANSWER and NION in anti-war demonstrations and it is a co-founder of the Independent Progressive Politics Network (IPPN), formed after 9/11to oppose the war on terror. The party platform is no mere set of environmental policy proposals. It seeks a socialist America based on the principles of "community-based economics" and "true-cost pricing." Its 2004 draft platform proposes to cut the defense budget in half, phases out all foreign military bases "not specifically functioning under a U.N. resolution," prohibits covert action and foreign arms sales, bans land mines and chemical and biological weapons stockpiling, and supports allowing annual visits by "foreign teams" for "verification purposes." Current U.S. policies in Iraq and Israel would be completely overturned and made subject to U.N. oversight.

In 2004 the Green Party did not endorse Ralph Nader, but it did welcome his independent bid for president as a complement to its own election efforts. Since they share the same ideological interpretation of the causes of the war, Greens see Nader as another voice on the left. Like Nader, the party believes the war in Iraq is fueled by the greed of corporate America.

The Greens are complemented by Code Pink, a women's group no less Marxist than the others. Code Pink ladies dress primly in pink and carry pink umbrellas when they stage their candlelight vigils or sit-ins in congressional offices. But looks deceive. The group is an off-shoot of ties formed in the mid-1980's when Medea Benjamin met Leslie Cagan. Benjamin was then a project coordinator for the pro-Sandinista Institute for Food and Development Policy (also known as Food First) while Cagan was coordinating marches against the Contras (and now coordinates United for Peace and Justice marches against George Bush).

In the 1990's Benjamin founded the group Global Exchange, which attacks free trade policy. The 1999 anti-globalization riots in Seattle were a high point for it. In 2000 she was the Green Party's candidate for the U.S. Senate in California. During this time Cagan was urging support for Castro's Cuba, managing David Dinkins' mayoral campaign, and serving on the board of the Astrea National Lesbian Action Foundation. Code Pink co-founder Jodie Evans was on the board of Rainforest Action Network (RAN), whose co-founder Mike Roselle earlier worked for Greenpeace, Earth First!, and the Ruckus Society, all groups that engage in violence to achieve their ends.

There are a reported 100 Code Pink chapters worldwide that have been on the frontlines since the start of the war in Iraq. Their mission is to incorporate the larger women's movement into peace protests. Code Pink's "Call to Action" takes advantage of this link:

"We call on women around the world to rise up and oppose the war in Iraq. We call on grandmothers, sisters and daughters, on workers, students, teachers, healers, artists, singers, poets and every ordinary outraged woman willing to be outrageous for peace. Women have been the guardians of life—not because we are better or purer or more innately nurturing then men, but because the men have busied themselves making war. Because of our responsibility to the next generation, because of our own love for our families and communities and this country that we are a part of, we understand the love of a mother in Iraq for her children, and the driving desire of that child for life."

Under the "love of a mother" banner Code Pink relentlessly organizes anti-war protest. In 2003-2004 it reports holding a four-month daily vigil in front of the White House and a march on Washington on March 8, International Women's Day. It sent a delegation to Baghdad to meet Iraqi women (Jan. 24-Feb. 4, 2004) and sponsored a signature "pink slip" action, "firing" Administration officials and the media who are "not doing their job." When U.S. troops attacked insurgents in Falluja in November 2004, Code Pink requested contributions to send medical assistance to the "people" of Falluja.

MoveOn.org

The anti-war organization least burdened by an embarrassing history of past communist affiliations is MoveOn.org. It was founded in 1998 by a married couple, Silicon Valley entrepreneurs Wes Boyd and Joan Blades, to protest the impending impeachment of President Bill Clinton, but took off during the Bush presidency. MoveOn can legitimately claim to have discovered how to use the power of the Internet to enlist and mobilize grassroots activists in politics and generate millions of dollars from small-dollar donors.

MoveOn exists primarily through cyberspace interactions. Its size and influence cannot be measured in conventional terms (staff, offices and endowments). In 2003 and 2004 it was a premier rallying point for anti-war activists opposed to the Bush Administration's policies in Iraq. Using the instant communication of the "web," it quickly amassed a membership of 1.8 million and raised a record $40 million. But MoveOn does not rely solely on small donors. After he saw what MoveOn could accomplish, billionaire George Soros contributed $2.5 million.

MoveOn opposed the U.S. attack on the Taliban in Afghanistan after 9/11, warning "If we retaliate by bombing Kabul and kill people oppressed by the Taliban, we become like the terrorists we oppose." It organized an e-mail petition that was signed by 500,000 people worldwide. In February 2003 it jammed congressional switchboards with hundreds of thousands of phone calls against the impending war in Iraq. A 22 year-old activist, Eli Pariser, became MoveOn's most visible spokesman. Using the web, he created a virtual march on Washington against the Iraq war. MoveOn then turned to politics, helping former Vermont Governor Howard Dean whose presidential candidacy bypassed the Democratic establishment. After Dean's campaign imploded, MoveOn re-focused its attacks on Bush, the Republican party and the war on terror.

Despite its many successes, some MoveOn tactics have

backfired. A nationwide Internet contest to select a "Bush in 30 seconds" advertisement went beyond the pale when a photo of the president morphed into Adolph Hitler on the MoveOn website. "What were war crimes in 1945" it declared, "is foreign policy in 2003." Jewish leaders like Rabbi Marvin Heir of the Wiesenthal Center called the ads "shameful"; Jack Rosen, president of the American Jewish Congress, found them "morally outrageous."

According to a Capital Research Center analysis, MoveOn has a unique capacity to "raise money and raise it fast." Said journalist Don Hazen, MoveOn's membership is "mostly white, highly educated, computer savvy... and willing to give dough." In October 2002 its political action committee raised $700,000 for Paul Wellstone's reelection after the Minnesota Senator voted against the Iraq war resolution. In November 2003 MoveOn used its database to raise $500,000 in five hours to distribute an anti-Bush ad. It raised the same amount in one day against California gubernatorial candidate Arnold Schwarzenegger and $800,000 in 48 hours on behalf of the Democratic Party in Texas. "MoveOn dwarfs everything in the progressive space," Hazen emphasized.

MoveOn's political base is broader and less radical than other groups in the movement. Shortly after 9/11 MoveOn proposed that foreign aid would deal with terrorism better than military action. According to *New Republic* editor Peter Beinart, "in recent years it seems to have largely lost interest in any agenda for fighting terrorism at all," preferring to criticize the war's effect on civil liberties.

When *New York Times* writer George Packer questioned why MoveOn would provide aid and comfort to terrorists and Communist dictators by supporting ANSWER's March 2003 demonstrations, Eli Pariser replied, "I'm personally against defending Slobodan Milosevic and calling North Korea a socialist heaven, but it's just not relevant right now." By adopting a "big tent" towards the far left, MoveOn has made a tacit alliance with it.

Protesting Republicans and George Bush

March 20, 2004 was the kick-off date for ANSWER's planned

"Summer of Protest and Resistance." As ANSWER assembled endorsements from over 1,500 U.S. supporters, it mobilized hundreds of thousands of demonstrators against the Democratic and Republican National Conventions.

ANSWER's "national actions" after the conventions included October marches for immigrant and workers rights in Los Angeles and Washington. The year of protest culminated with a Washington, DC Counter-Inaugural on January 20, 2005, an event that presages further protest actions against the Bush Admini-stration as it consolidates its November electoral triumph.

Anti-war groups promised impressive protests at the Democratic and Republican National Conventions. However, the demonstrations in the host cities, Boston and New York City, proved to be anticlimactic. The organizers appear to have decided that disruptive protests would backfire and hurt their cause.

Democratic and Republican convention officials responded differently to the prospect of violent disturbances. The Democrats, meeting at Boston's Fleet Center in late July, made sure that anti-war groups were confined to a "free-speech zone"—a large wire cage with one entrance and one exit topped by razor wire. The cage was built for no more than 400 protesters and it enclosed a lot under Boston's elevated train tracks, tucked away from access to the Fleet Center by a maze of service roads, train tracks and a parking lot for buses and media trucks. "The area looks a little silly, to be honest with you," said an official of the National Lawyers Guild, which filed a legal challenge. "No one will be heard, and the area is just too small." Precisely.

When the Republicans met in New York City's Madison Square Garden one month later the anti-war movement seemed back on track. Over 200,000 protesters had the run of the city—only Central Park was off-limits—on the Sunday evening before the convention opened. However, Leslie Cagan, who directed protest sponsor United for Peace and Justice, deemed the protesters "orderly" and "peaceful." The press treated the demonstrators as interesting and colorful. The front page of the *Washington Post* found the mood exciting:

Hundreds of police officers in riot gear lined the sidewalks, SWAT

39

vans idled, and police helicopters whirred overhead. But the protest was as peaceful as it was vast. More than 200,000 demonstrators, according to a police estimate, packed dozens of blocks along Seventh Avenue and snaked down side streets.

…While passions ran high, the mood was often celebratory. As the marchers inched along Seventh Avenue, New Yorkers waved from windows and rooftops, and three gay couples enjoying Sunday brunch at the Eros Café in the Chelsea neighborhood raised glasses of orange juice to salute.

….“We couldn’t be happier,” said Leslie Cagan, the march’s lead organizer. “People came to say no to the Bush agenda with all the diversity of our neighborhoods. We won the streets of New York.”

The press could see no suggestion of radicalism or violence, only concern for free speech and democracy.

- “People are recognizing they need to vote with their feet. They need to be out in the streets,” said a national organizer for Not In Our Name.

- Said Brian Becker of ANSWER, “We feel very heartened by the massive turnout this week. It gave the anti-war movement a great gust of wind in its sails.”

- UPJ’s Leslie Cagan agreed: “I think people are coming off of this week feeling very strong, very empowered… So hopefully people will go back into their neighborhoods and be inspired by this whole week and keep the action going.”

- Code Pink’s Andrea Buffa recalled a teenager who joined the marchers: “She’s 14 and she’s going to be an activist for the rest of her life because of what she participated in this week.”

The 3500 Republican delegates ignored the protesters, even when they deliberately crowded entry and exit approaches to Madison Square Garden. An official RNC handout on “How to Deal with Protesters” advised: “Do not engage protesters in debate. The protesters are here to get media coverage. Debating them simply provides fodder for the TV camera and the press. Be patient. Protesters want to make it harder to get around New York. Give yourself extra time.”

Crowd size estimates varied. The police thought there were 200,000 protesters early in the week, but *USA Today* estimated a "half million or so." By any account the demonstration was the largest convention-related protest in American history.

But there was little violence, nothing to compare to the 1968 Democratic convention. Mayor Bloomberg's police force was not Mayor Daley's. By week's end, the NYPD had efficiently arrested over 1,800 protesters, nearly three times the number arrested by Chicago police in 1968. About 150 were arrested near Ground Zero for taking part in a prohibited "death march" sponsored by the War Resisters League. Three hundred marched up Broadway and about fifty staged a "die-in" blocks from the convention. In all, at least 200 members of the War Resisters League were arrested during the week.

Another 1,000 demonstrated outside Fox News headquarters in a "shut-up-a thon" against talk show host Bill O'Reilly and Fox's pro-war news coverage. For over two hours they chanted in unison "Shut the Fox up." Said one, "The beef with Fox News is the more you watch, the less you know. It is very important to know weapons of mass destruction were never found in Iraq."

Hooded anti-war protesters threw fake blood and heckled TV host Chris Matthews as he broadcast live from Herald Square. But a spokesman for United for Peace and Justice (UPJ) differentiated those arrested from most others, noting "Our event was peaceful, and I hope that the media and the public kept those arrests in perspective."

The failure of mainstream press coverage to discuss the political background and ideology of the protest organizers extended even to a pro-administration news outlet like the *Washington Times*. It did no more than identify UPJ as a group "which claims an anti-Bush agenda." *USA Today* said the protests were successful "in focusing attention on the anti-war sentiment in the country and providing a boost to a movement they say will continue long after the Republican convention."

By treating the anti-war movement as a news event rather than as a well-organized and long-established political movement, the media failed to fully inform Americans about these groups. War protests are tactics. But more important is the organizers' strategy to change society and politics.

Chapter 2

BEHIND THE FRONT LINES

ANSWER, United for Peace and Justice, and Not In Our Name organize today's anti-war protests and marches. They are the front-line organizations. It is their job to figure out the timing and street logistics of anti-war protest marches and decide how to handle the middle class suburbanites, radicalized students and anarchist street kids who join them. The groups come up with the sound bites their spokesmen use to interpret anti-war protest to the media. And they argue with each other over whose interpretation is most politically correct.

However, behind the front-line groups is another layer of organization. Here you find the lawyers and civil rights organizations that keep protest leaders out of prison and argue for putting restraints on the government's ability to act. You also find the think-tanks that market their arguments to the news media, and the grantmakers that fund their work. Lastly, you find the academics and writers who develop the ideas to explain the justice of the protesters' cause and the injustice of the government's.

The intellectual infrastructure supporting anti-war protest groups typically appeals to the liberal tradition of freedom and due process of law. Sometimes it invokes the socialist tradition of class solidarity. Only on occasion is it so forthright as to justify civil disruption by advocating violence, conspiracy and subversion. This chapter identifies some of the key players.

National Lawyers Guild

The National Lawyers Guild (NLG) is no stranger to radical protest. Since 1937 NLG has been supplying legal counsel to Communist and other left-wing causes. It remains the principal legal front for radical groups that help the terrorists and their sympathizers in their war on America. At some point most anti-American, anti-capitalist, anti-war and anti-imperialist causes on the far left fall into its embrace.

NLG is deeply involved in assisting the major anti-war groups. It helped co-found Not in Our Name, and during the Republican convention it worked with members of the Workers World Party and International ANSWER to defend protesters and protest police presence. It also supplied legal assistance to groups such as the Revolutionary Communist Party, the All-African Peoples Revolutionary Party, Refuse and Resist!, and the International League of Peoples' Struggle. After the convention it sued New York City for false police arrests and detentions. NLG lawyers also represent U.S. army troops in Iraq who in December 2004 sued the federal government over its "stop-loss" policy extending enlistments.

Founded as an alternative to the once-conservative American Bar Association, NLG says it is "dedicated to the need for basic change in the structure of our political and economic system." Currently it has 4000 members in over forty local chapters, a national executive committee of regional vice presidents, and a New York City national headquarters. Twenty one NLG committees set policy on the Middle East, Cuba, the death penalty, immigration, racism, sexism, drug law, military law, "mass defense" (i.e. counsel for demonstrators), labor, prison law, and international affairs. Over ninety law schools have student Guild chapters. The Kansas City-based National Lawyers Guild Foundation provides assistance to local chapters. It reported to the IRS 2001 revenues of $1,142,980 (including a $1 million gift from an unnamed donor) and $305,333 in 2002.

Former NLG staffer Bernadine Dohrn was a member of the terrorist Weather Underground in the 1970's; like Angela Davis she too was once a fugitive on the FBI's "10 Most Wanted" list, and she is currently a professor of law at Northwestern University.

Explaining the Guild's role in helping the modern Left, Dohrn notes that NLG lawyers embrace "a huge array of social issues. From immigration and labor, ecology, international law, women's rights, children's rights and so on. It is very much in the tradition of the 1960's grassroots organization, where local chapters work away on their own priorities but are a part of a broader network and coalition."

In the 1930's NLG attracted New Deal liberals, labor lawyers, and independent leftists as well as core Communists. But the die was cast at its third annual convention, when NLG delegates refused to go on record opposing dictatorship and supporting democracy, a proposition they regarded as "divisive." After World War II NLG adopted a clearly pro-Communist line. It opposed the Truman Doctrine, the Marshall Plan, NATO, U.S. opposition to Communist China, domestic loyalty oaths, the FBI, and legislation allowing the Justice Department to monitor Communist fronts. Guild members represented the "Hollywood 10" screenwriters and Julius and Ethel Rosenberg.

NLG membership dropped to about 2,000 after a 1950 House Committee on Un-American Activities "Report on the National Lawyers Guild: Legal Bulwark of the Communist Party." It noted the Guild's attack on "the Federal Bureau of Investigation [as] part of an overall Communist strategy aimed at weakening our nation's defenses against the international Communist conspiracy." The report recommended Guild membership be defined as "subversive" and members barred from federal employment.

However, in the 1960's the Guild took advantage of the changing and more radical political climate. It attracted a new following of white and black radicals (including future Ohio congressman John Conyers). NLG members supported radical student politics and the civil rights movement and opposed the Vietnam War. Guild lawyers defended anti-war protestors and draft evaders. They offered legal help to rioters at the 1968 Democratic Convention and members of the militant Black Panther Party.

By the late 1970's NLG moved further left, making direct attacks on the system of criminal law. One Guild president, Paul Harris, quoted Lenin to the effect that a "legal struggle" must parallel illegal militant actions to make a successful revolution. He came up with a theory of "guerilla law" and devised a "black rage" defense. Another president, Doris Brin Walker, proclaimed herself "proud to be a member of the Communist Party."

In the 1970's Guild lawyers represented the terrorists of the Weather Underground and prisoners involved in the notorious 1971 Attica uprising. The Guild had overseas clients—the Palestine Liberation Organization, the Viet Cong, the African National Congress, pro-Soviet Angolan and Mozambican factions, the Puerto Rican FALN, and the Philippine New People's Army. NLG membership was over 7,000 by the mid-1980's. The Guild's Communist clients included the Sandinistas in Nicaragua and the FMLN in El Salvador. However, the collapse of the Soviet Union in 1991 was a setback for the Guild, which never lost its affection for the USSR.

Contrary to popular belief, the "neocoms" soldier on. Guild member Chip Berlet colorfully depicted NLG meetings in 1999:

The cacophony at some [Guild] meetings makes Star Wars seem like a minimalist film. I have chaired committee meetings with debates featuring cadres from Leninist, Trotskyist, Stalinist, and Maoist groups, along with Marxists, anarchists, libertarians, and progressive independents-interacting with a preponderance of reluctant Democrats-all intertwined with multiple alternate identities as lawyers, legal workers, labor organizers, tribal sovereignty activists, civil liberties and civil rights advocates, environmentalists, feminists, gay men and lesbians, and people of color.

The core of NLG's strategy is an assault on U.S. law. It promotes mass civil disobedience, protects those who challenge legal authority, and embraces subversive groups and causes. Worse, it aids terrorists within the U.S. homeland.

In particular, the Guild has targeted the War on Terror. The Guild's formal projects include a National Police Accountability Project, which thwarts police attempts to apprehend suspected terrorists, and a National Immigration Project, which interrupts U.S. border enforcement and immigration laws. NLG lawyers abet opposition to the USA PATRIOT Act, attack the use of military tribunals, and would force the federal government to reveal the names of detained aliens. NLG lawyers justify lawbreaking. According to the Guild,

Under well accepted general principles of criminal law applicable in every U.S. jurisdiction, otherwise technically illegal acts may be justified by the necessity of preventing a greater wrong or danger—form of self-defense or defense of others. In this case there is ample legal necessity and justification for non-violent resistance to these illegal and immensely destructive, murderous actions by the top officials of the U.S. government.

In NLG eyes the United States, not Al Qaeda, is the war criminal. Recent Guild flyers, posters and CDs advise immigrants and suspected terrorists, often in Arabic and Farsi, that "Talking to the FBI or other agents can be dangerous" and "You do not have to talk to the police, FBI, INS or any other investigation."

The Guild increasingly attacks government efforts to fight terrorism. In a February 10, 2004 case, NLG lawyers forced federal prosecutors to withdraw a subpoena demanding that Drake University hand over information on participants in a November 2003 anti-war rally. In a press release, NLG executive director Heidi Boghosian stated, "This is a complete retreat by the U.S. Attorney and an unequivocal victory for the National Lawyers Guild and the peace movement." One defendant told reporters, "The withdraw of the subpoenas was a victory, but unfortunately the war gets more disgusting. Hopefully, people are beginning to learn that the National Guard fighting in Iraq is not making us free. Freedom is something that has to be fought for here in the streets of America. We are the people fighting the real terrorists."

Also in February 2004, NLG investigated a U.S. Army attempt to gather information on a University of Texas conference on Islam. NLG president Michael Avery warned: "It appears that the government is stepping up surveillance of innocent activity at academic institutions... An element of racial profiling is present in this case, given the Muslim content of this particular event. Government spying on student conferences has no place in a free society."

The Guild-related law firm Rabinowitz, Boudin, Standard, Krinsky, and Lieberman is actually legal counsel for the Castro regime, and NLG lawyers have defended Cuban government interests. The Guild's Cuba subcommittee has been trying for years to normalize U.S.-Cuban relations and to end the travel restrictions and the economic embargo. NLG currently represents the notorious "Cuban Five" who have been convicted of espionage. Guild president Bruce Nestor says the imprisoned spies were only "defending their country from long-documented acts of terror attacks by organizations in Miami."

Center for Constitutional Rights

On September 22, 2004 the Justice Department announced that it would release Yaser Esam Hamdi, an American citizen captured with Taliban units in Afghanistan in 2001 and held since then as an "enemy combatant" in Guantanamo. Many saw Hamdi's case, which was decided by the Supreme Court in *Hamdi v. Rumsfeld,* as a clash between U.S. anti-terror laws and civil liberties. Hamdi was transferred to Saudi Arabia where he spent most of his life.

However, the "peace movement" heralded Hamdi's court victory as an anti-terror setback. Hamdi's defense was engineered by the New York City-based Center for Constitutional Rights (CRC), another radical left legal front for the peace movement.

CCR was founded in 1966 by a group of leftist lawyers led by William Kunstler (1919-1995), lead defense attorney in the trial of the "Chicago Seven" activists charged with inciting riots at the Democratic National Convention in 1968. It advertises itself as the nation's "premiere" legal institution for the advance of human rights and social and racial justice. In reality, it is, in the words of *FrontPage magazine.com* author John Perazzo, a "Fifth Column law factory, part of the same political left that has spent decades portraying America as a racist, corrupt, arrogant violator of human rights both at home and abroad."

The Center reported revenue of $2,407,412 in 2002 and $915,308 (including $112,0000 in court awards and legal fees) in 2003.

The record of CCR positions since its founding, and including its conduct of the Hamdi case, supports this description. During the Vietnam War, CCR supported the Viet Cong and North Vietnam, and it opposed the Reagan Administration's anti-Communist policies that led to the downfall of Soviet Communism. After 9/11

CCR denounced Bush Administration efforts to protect U.S. borders and wage an anti-terror war in Afghanistan and Iraq. It puts a "blame America" spin on all its legal arguments, whether in support of illegal aliens, taking action against Homeland Security policies, or filing suit against "racial profiling."

Legal director Barbara Olshansky argues that the defense of rights requires CCR to develop "litigation to challenge this campaign of harassment." CCR president Michael Ratner charges that U.S. policies are the root cause of global terror, noting that the U.S. "must make fundamental changes in its foreign policies [which] continue to anger people throughout the region, and to fertilize the ground where terrorists of the future will take root." Ratner's solution to 9/11? He would take an expedited case to the United Nations and then try the suspects in a world court.

Many CCR supporters have long histories on the Left. Attorney Lynne Stewart began her career in the 1970's defending members of the terrorist Weather Underground. Two decades later she represented the blind sheik Omar Abdul Rahman, who in 1993 masterminded the first terror attack against the World Trade Center. A decade later Stewart found herself under indictment for exploiting her attorney-client confidentiality privileges: she is charged with sending messages from the imprisoned cleric to his terrorist supporters in Egypt. Stewart is now defended by two attorney colleagues: NLG attorney Susan Tipograph, herself once accused of helping a Puerto Rican terrorist escape from jail, and Stanley Cohen, a legal and political advocate for Hamas. Stewart is proud of her Communist beliefs, but flavors them with made-in-America commentary: "I don't believe in anarchistic violence, but directed violence... When the revolution comes to this country, it'll be as American as apple pie and baseball."

With the release of Hamdi, CCR's work seems to have paid off. "This is tremendously embarrassing to the government," CCR attorney Shayana Kadidal told reporters.

Radical Islamic Groups

The vast majority of American Muslims oppose radical and

totalitarian ideas, and they avoid contact with extremist groups. But Muslim extremist organizations are a "clear and present danger." Information is hard to come by but there is evidence of growing ties linking radical Islam to the anti-war movement, a potential alliance that could pose the greatest post 9/11 threat to American security. It's hard to imagine that religious fundamentalists would make common cause with secular, indeed, atheist activists. But a union of sectarian American Marxist revolutionaries to a Muslim fringe is in the making and could produce major social disruptions. With the means and will to destroy a society they hate, that combination of forces is a real and immediate danger.

The group **Focus on American and Arab Interests and Relations (FAAIR)** was organized in the Detroit suburb of Southfield soon after 9/11 by two Iraqi expatriates, Mohammed Alomari and Muthana al-Hanooti. FAAIR promises "to promote fair policies and a better understanding of the issues pertaining to the Arab World." In fact, FAAIR is in league with America's enemies.

Alomari says America's presence in Iraq is a war against a "besieged nation" and that the president makes excuses that run "the entire gamut of war pretexts, everything from fighting terrorism and weapons of mass destruction to establishing democracies around the world." On his website, www.faair.org, Alomari says the Bush Administration is dominated by a cabal of 32 Jewish Americans who wage war in Iraq for Israel's sake. He demands the ouster of a complicit Secretary of State Colin Powell. Alomari's essay, "Twelve Years of Siege on Iraq," is a reference to U.S. policies. Located on the FAAIR website, it is part of his larger study, "The Blockade and Destruction of Iraq: Crimes Against Humanity."

FAAIR leads a coalition of some 150 groups that have been enlisted to engage in "nonviolent defiance of U.S. law." One of these groups is the Campaign of Conscience for the Iraqi People (CCIP), which urges Americans to break U.S. law by shipping supplies to Iraq. On its website, FAAIR says it's never too late to donate illegal contraband. CCIP was formed by two groups that were once part of the traditional peace movement: the American Friends Service Committee and the Fellowship of Reconciliation. They are now reliable allies of the left.

FAAIR also has ties with the Iraq Action Coalition (IAC), "an independent grassroots coalition dedicated to providing information on the consequences of the blockade of Iraq and providing assistance to the Iraqi people." Founded in 1993 by Dr. Rania Masri, a 33 year-old Arab-American, IAC speakers fan out to U.S. campuses explaining how to combat the "continuing war against Iraq." Masri, an outspoken opponent of "profiling," declares that in America "simply looking Middle Eastern has become a crime." She has condemned the search for al Qaeda and Osama bin Laden, claiming that the charges against them for 9/11 have been trumped-up by the Bush Administration.

FAAIR also associates with major U.S. peace groups, especially Peace Action, an amalgam of two Cold War era organizations, Committee for a Sane Nuclear Policy (SANE) and the Nuclear Weapons Freeze Campaign (FREEZE). Together with two affiliates, the grantmaking Peace Action Education Fund (2002 revenue $365,471) and the Student Peace Action Network (SPAN), Peace Action claims a membership of 85,000, with 27 state affiliates and over 100 local chapters, a claim that would make it the nation's largest peace group. (Rania Masri is a national board member of North Carolina Peace Action.)

Peace Action hasn't changed much since the Cold War—it is still committed to the "abolition of nuclear weapons" and to what it calls a "peace-oriented economy." But by associating with an organization like FAAIR, Peace Action links itself to an enemy of the war on terror, one that claims Israel and the U.S. are the true "terrorists." "The biggest nuclear threat we now face," a SPAN associate wrote, "doesn't come from some rogue nation, but from the radical unilateralists within the Bush Administration."

Peace Action claims funding from foundations like the New World Foundation (which Hillary Clinton chaired in 1987-1988). Other funding sources include The Ploughshares Fund ($57,500 to three affiliates in 2002) Scherman Foundation, Lifebridge Foundation and Tides Foundation ($46,000 in 2002, $18,000 in 2003, including $1000 designated for United for Peace and Justice).

A second U.S.-based Islamic extremist group is the **Council on American Islamic Relations (CAIR)**, which has lead anti-American demonstrations and is a member of the ANSWER coalition. CAIR was founded in 1994 with an interest-free loan from the Saudi Islamic Development Bank. Although it portrays itself an Arab political lobby opposed to discrimination, academic and media critics say it is a front group for the Muslim fundamentalist Wahhabi sect. Its leaders repeatedly embrace terrorist groups like Hamas, which CAIR's Executive Director, Nihad Awad, is on record as supporting: "I am a supporter of the Hamas movement," he told one audience.

CAIR's advocacy role is bipolar: it publicly defends Arab rights while police and FBI evidence shows that CAIR has defended and financed terror groups and actions. After September 2003 hearings, the Senate's Judiciary subcommittee on terrorism, technology and homeland security issued a report, "Two Years After 9/11: Connecting the Dots," which demonstrated the influence of Saudi money and the Wahhabi sect on many Muslim political groups in the U.S. Awad and CAIR chairman Omar Ahmed refused invitations from the subcommittee to testify.

A number of CAIR staffers have been charged with conspiracy and/or abetting terrorism.

- CAIR civil rights coordinator Ismail Royer was arrested in January 2003 for his role in a "Virginia jihad network." The indictment charged that he stocked munitions and arms and aided in the planning a "violent jihad on behalf of Muslims in Kashmir, Chechnya, the Philippines and other countries and territories..."

- CAIR director of community affairs Bassem K. Khafagi, plead guilty for his involvement with The Islamic Assembly of North America (IANA), which advocates violence against the U.S. Other IANA officials were arrested earlier after FBI raids on their headquarters in Ypsilanti, Michigan. One of them, Saudi-born Sami al Hussayen, ran websites propagating radical Islam.

The September 2003 Senate hearing traced money from Saudi Arabia to CAIR. Concluded committee chairman Senator John Kyl (R-AZ), "A small group of organizations based in the U.S. with Saudi backing and support, is well-advanced in its four-decade effort to control Islam in America—from mosques, universities and community centers to our prisons and even to our military.

Moderate Muslims, who love America and want to be part of our great country are being forced out of those institutions." Senator Charles Schumer (D-NY) pointed to CAIR, noting that absent CAIR leaders had "intimate links with Hamas [and] ties to terrorism." Even Senator Richard Durbin (D-IL), known for his soft line on CAIR, reluctantly concluded that CAIR is "unusual in its extreme rhetoric and its associations with groups that are suspect."

Muslim Public Affairs Council (MPAC) is a communications front for radical Islam and jihad violence. Mideast expert Daniel Pipes has observed that the difference between MPAC and CAIR is that MPAC declares itself "moderate," disavows foreign funding and is based in Los Angeles. CAIR has accepted at least $250,000 from Saudi Arabia to buy land for its Washington, D.C. headquarters.

MPAC too has Saudi backing and maintains close ties to CAIR. Just hours after the morning attacks of 9/11, MPAC director Salam al-Marayati issued a statement claiming Israel was the perpetrator:

"If we're going to look at suspects, we should look to the groups that benefit the most from these kinds of incidents, and I think that we should put the state of Israel on the suspect list because I think this diverts attention from what's happening in the Palestinian territories so that they can go on with their aggression and occupation and apartheid policies."

In February 2003 MPAC vice chairman Aslam Abdullah went so far as to suggest that radical Islam could liberate Americans:

"Americans realize that many in the country have started speaking up. The political Zionists want to silence them before they become louder. They realize that young Muslim Americans are in the forefront of this movement of liberating America from the influence of racist policies of political Zionists. They want to silence them."

These extreme statements are typical to MPAC. In a 1999 position paper MPAC justified Hezbollah's 1983 bombing of the Marine barracks in Lebanon that killed 241 U.S. Marines: "This attack, for all the pain it caused, was not in a strict sense, a terrorist operation. It was a military operation, producing no civilian casualties—exactly the kind of attack that Americans might have lauded had it been directed against Washington's enemies."

Fortunately, law enforcement authorities are uncovering more information about these groups—and with startling results. For instance, until recently few people understood the character of the **American Muslim Council (AMC),** formed in 1990 by Abdurahman Alamoudi, a veteran operative for terrorist fronts backed by Saudi funding. He presented himself to the public and to the Bush Administration as an Islamic civil rights advocate. When FBI director Robert Mueller addressed AMC's national convention in 2002, he gave the group a legitimacy money can't buy. Official FBI press releases called the organization "mainstream."

But Alamoudi was an enthusiastic supporter of Hezbollah and Hamas. Former AMC executive board president Jamir Abdullah Al-Amin has twice appeared on the FBI's "Most Wanted" list (under his Vietnam-era name, H. "Rap" Brown). AMC executive director Kit Gage works full-time with the National Lawyers Guild. University of South Florida professor Sami Al –Arian, arrested on terrorism charges in February 2003, was once an AMC president.

The ax fell on Alamoudi and AMC in 2004. On July 30, Alamoudi plead guilty in U.S. district court in Alexandria, Virginia, to illegally moving monies from Libya in an elaborate plot to assassinate Saudi Crown Prince Abdullah. Court records show Alamoudi was the go-between among conspirators in Libya, the U.S. and Saudi Arabia. His guilty plea marks the end of his influence as a Muslim "advocate" who once successfully courted high-level U.S. officials. The AMC is now shut down.

With vigorous follow-up the U.S. government should be able to undermine terrorism's domestic Islamic base, including the many charities, think-tanks and companies whose money laundering and tax fraud supports terrorist groups at home and abroad.

Institute for Policy Studies

The Institute for Policy Studies (IPS), founded in 1963 by New Left radicals Marcus Raskin and Richard Barnet, is the Godfather of left-wing think tanks. Tap into a leftist idea or organization and it's likely you can trace at least some of its roots to IPS, which for over 40 years has provided arguments for those opposing U.S. power in the world. IPS is neither pacifist nor utopian; it has consistently dedicated itself to an ideological revolutionary socialism that ex-leftist David Horowitz labels "Trotskyite."

Based in Washington, D.C., IPS (2002 revenues: $2,859,594) defends the rallies for Palestinian terrorists and provides the intellectual cover for leftist disruptions. Its extensive programs and publications on the techniques of activist organizing assures IPS an important role on the political scene in 2004 and beyond.

In September 2003, just four month after the defeat of Saddam Hussein, IPS reviewed the future of the global peace movement at a forum in Jakarta, Indonesia. The review, called the Jakarta Peace Consensus (JPC), proposed to establish the following strategic and institutional structures:

- an Occupation Watch Center in Iraq;
- International Peoples War Crimes Tribunal on Iraq;
- international campaign against U.S. military bases;
- international campaign against corporate looters and war profiteers;
- international conference in Baghdad;
- antiwar assembly during the next World Social Forum;
- a 2004 "World Says No to Bush" campaign to prevent the President's reelection.

This is obviously very ambitious, but IPS has not hesitated to push for a global protest coalition. Already the War Crimes Tribunal project has mobilized lawyers and policy experts. According to the IPS website, the tribunal organizers are determined that "it will not just be a mock trial but an attempt to push the frontiers of international law to promote justice... The goal is to mobilize the best crop of internationally recognized jurists and prosecutors and to painstakingly assemble the most solid and most fool-proof pieces of evidence by the expertise of lawyers and testimonies." The prominent leftist international law scholar Richard Falk has endorsed the tribunal: "I think this venture could have a great impact. It is important to be sensitive to efforts to discredit the venture as an unconstituted kangaroo court."

The IPS board includes former IPS director Robert Borosage, author Barbara Ehrenreich, Texas activist Frances Farenthold, singer Harry Belafonte and *Nation* magazine editor Katrina vanden Heuvel.

"Peace Studies"

The simplistic idea of an institution dedicated exclusively to promoting peace has long intrigued pacifist and left-leaning anti-war groups. Unfortunately, this kind of thinking supports the latest academic fad. The phenomenon known as "peace studies" is now pervasive on college campuses.

The idea of a separate government focus on "peace" can be traced to 1793, when the pacifist Benjamin Rush proposed a cabinet-rank Peace Department. A modern version surfaced in 2003 when Rep. Dennis Kucinich (D-OH) proposed a Secretary of Peace to oversee and overcome domestic and foreign violence. Kucinich introduced a bill that received 46 co-sponsors, all Democrats. Proposals such as Kuchinich's attract professors and students who believe peace can be achieved by a "political will" that can be a substitute for national security.

The first program in peace studies was set up at Indiana's pacifist-run Manchester College in 1948, but programs and curricula have expanded along with America's engagement with the world. Today over 250 American colleges and universities have a concentration or degree program. That these programs are heavily ideological is demonstrated in *Peace Studies: A Critical Survey* (1984) by Caroline Cox and Roger Scruton. The authors leave little doubt that Marxist or quasi-Marxist assumptions underlie the discipline, which is a powerful intellectual force behind anti-war activism.

In fairness, some peace programs are intellectually rigorous.

They draw upon social psychology and models of business negotiation, and offer a Hobbesian and "realist" perspective on violence and force. Most, however, simply enlarge upon Marxist, feminist and race-conscious interpretations of American society.

Columbia University's International Center for Cooperation and Conflict Resolution, whose website links class, sex and race to warfare, is a typical example. "Societal issues such as racism, sexism and class conflict must be openly and effectively addressed [to] demonstrate non-violent means of fostering social change and building a peaceful culture." At the University of California, Berkeley several peace study professors saw the 9/11 attacks as igniting an American backlash of hate crimes and race riots.

Peace studies programs during the Vietnam war era helped mobilize the campus anti-war movement. It's happening again. Israeli scholar Gerald Steinberg concludes:

Peace education, like many other topics in the social sciences, is susceptible to the tension between the academic objective of value-free analysis, on the one hand, and particularist as well as highly subjective advocacy, on the other... Furthermore, in an idealist framework in which all use of military force by state actors is essentially anathema, and which is strongly influenced by external and non-academic and often ideological factors, the framework of peace studies has often been exploited for attacks against specific countries, specifically the U.S. and Israel. The policies of both countries are routinely subject to condemnation... and the context in which force is used in self-defense is often ignored. In a major departure from academic norms or conduct, and in a manner that undermines the credibility of peace studies, faculty members encourage their students to participate in political rallies, boycotts and similar activities.

Sources of Funding

Herbert Romerstein, long–recognized as one of America's top experts on internal security, recently addressed the question of funding the far left. Romerstein, a veteran investigator for the House Permanent Select Committee on Intelligence and former head of the U.S. Information Agency Office to Counter Soviet

Active Measures, spoke with J. Michael Waller of *Insight* magazine (March 4–17, 2003). He noted, "There's no such thing as a spontaneous demonstration."

Romerstein believes the funding for anti-war and anti-Bush protests comes from the coffers of their principal organizer, the Workers World Party. He notes that "Workers World is totally subservient to North Korea. What we don't know is if there's money coming in." However, he suspects that WWP's close ties to North Korea make it likely that much of the current funding comes from Kim Il-jong.

The USA Patriot Act provides the legal justification for conducting secret operations against terrorist groups and groups supporting them. That's why groups look for "civil libertarian" grounds to stymie its implementation. WWP would be in violation of the Act and a legitimate target for investigation and sanctions if it receives funding from foreign sources, especially hostile governments. "No very radical group in the U.S.," Romerstein concluded, "has been able to exist for very long without direct foreign support."

Still, it is important to observe that covert funding is unnecessary to support the many programs and organizations that provide excuses for terrorists and arguments for opposing the war on terror. Any number of individuals, foundations and nonprofits fund the war on the war on terror. Writing in the online *Front Page* magazine (www.frontpagemag.com) author Ben Johnson notes that left-wing funding comes from a number of sources:

Inevitably, the large tax-exempt foundations fund the same radical personalities and groups. Their staff is invariably composed of the same far-Left activists (and a curiously high number of Clinton administration appointees). Ultimately, these inter-related organizations form one well-heeled, left-wing Brain Trust with literally billions of dollars at their disposal. These foundations are positioned to permanently shift our nation's political dialogue to the Left through their grant-making power.

George Soros is one person on the "must-see" list for every left-wing group. This white male European billionaire once denounced fat cat donors and demanded campaign finance reform. But in 2003 Soros changed his tune and contributed $10 million to set up America Coming Together (ACT) to defeat George Bush, whom he compared to Adolf Hitler. ACT is a so-called "527" independent expenditure political committee that can spend "soft money" contributions for political purposes. Soros supports other "527" groups (named after the section of the IRS code permitting them) as well as nonprofit think tanks and advocacy groups like the Center for American Progress (CAP), headed by former Clinton chief-of-staff John Podesta. CAP, which aims to rival the Heritage Foundation, received a $3 million gift from Soros.

Soros also funds anti-war activities through gifts from his Open Society Institute (OSI) (2002 assets $251 million). OSI insists that its philanthropy is separate from Soros' political activities, but it provides grants to such groups as Watchingjustice.org, a website dedicated to monitoring the Department of Justice. The director of the OSI-Washington office is veteran activist Morton Halperin, who has said of Attorney General John Ashcroft, "I think he's basically out of control."

OSI gave the **Tides Foundation** $13 million between 1997 and 2003. (The Foundation and its affiliated Tides Center also received more than $4 million from the Heinz Endowments, whose chairman is Teresa Heinz Kerry.) Tides is a unique go-between grantmaker that is organized to accept money from the respectable to give to the disreputable. A self-described "fiscal sponsor" of many radical peace groups, Tides has given grants to the Council on American Islamic Relations, National Lawyers Guild, Center on Constitutional Rights, and United for Peace and Justice. OSI independently gave $50,000 to the National Lawyers Guild in 2000 and over $120,000 to the Center for Constitutional Rights between 1998 and 2004.

The **Ford Foundation** (2002 assets—over $11 billion) typically ignores criticism of its giving. But it grew defensive when it found itself on the wrong side in the war on terror after giving $1.4 million to the Palestinian NGO Network (PNGO) a Palestinian political alliance of some 90 groups. When the groups stridently attacked the U.S. and Israel at the 2001 U.N. World Conference Against Racism in Durban, South Africa, their funding arrangements attracted Congress's attention. The possibility of oversight hearings led Ford and the Rockefeller Foundation to institute new guidelines requiring every grant recipient to demonstrate that its funding would not be used to support terrorism. The ACLU protested the new policy, and in October 2004 returned Ford grants, which totaled $1.1 million that year. The ACLU received $1.5 million from Ford in 2003 and $2.7 million in 2002.

Ford grants directly funded the Durban conference just two days before 9/11. The foundation also has given grants annually to groups like the Ploughshares Fund, the Tides Center, the American Friends Service Committee, the Lawyers Committee for Human Rights, and the Center for Constitutional Rights, all leftist opponents of the Bush Administration's Iraq policy. Ford gave the Ploughshares Fund more than $1million in 2003 to support anti-war activities. A grant-making organization that styles itself a "mutual fund for peace," Ploughshares in turn has made grants to the Carnegie Endowment, which supports handing off the war on terror to multilateral agencies, and the U.S. Campaign to Ban Land Mines, a policy the U.S. has rejected. Ford grants support *The Progressive* magazine, a harsh anti-war journal ($600,000 in 2003).

Ford gave over $5 million during the past three years to the Tides Center (2002 assets, $190 million), a spin-off of the Tides Foundation. The Center acts as an incubator for nonprofits, providing legal and fundraising support for groups that are too new or too small to have their own administrative apparatus. It has received over $26 million from Ford since 1990. Since 9/11 Tides has given more than $1.5 million to another anti-war group, Win Without War, which is led by former U.S. Rep. Tom Andrews (D-ME). It gave $50,000 in 2002 to September Eleventh Families for Peaceful Tomorrows, which has condemned the U.S. attack on Saddam Hussein's regime as "illegal, immoral and unjustified."

The Lawyers Committee for Human Rights (LCHR)—its new name is Human Rights First—has received about $1.6 million from The Ford Foundation over three years. It worries that the rights of human rights defenders are eroded by U.S. security policies. Ford Foundation contributions to the American Friends Service Committee were about $400,000 in 2002-2004. Ford gave the Center for Constitutional Rights about $225,000 in 2002-2004.

The **John D. and Catherine T. MacArthur Foundation** (2002 assets—$4 billion) is best known for its controversial "genius" grants, but it also underwrites activist groups and left-wing think tanks that produce studies opposing America's campaign against terror. It gave more than $400,000 in 1999-2000 to Global Exchange (a group co-founded by Code Pink's Medea Benjamin), which organized the 1999 Seattle demonstrations against the meeting of the World Trade Organization. In 2001 it gave $233,000 to the Institute for Policy Studies and over $300,000 to the Center for Defense Information. MacArthur also awarded the Aspen Institute $841,000 to study "global interdependence." That support will assist Aspen, which notes a growing gap between Bush policies and what it claims is the public's interest in having the U.S. participate in United Nations forums.

The Florence and John Schumann Foundation (recently renamed the **Schumann Center for Media and Democracy**) is a small foundation (2003 assets—$69 million). But under its president, PBS guru Bill Moyers (who also sits on the board of George Soros' OSI), it has an agenda that is sharply focused on pushing America to the left. It gave $332,000 to Ralph Nader's Public Citizen Foundation between 1995 and 2000. (Ford Foundation gave the Nader-founded group $450,000 in 2000.) Moyers enlisted pledges of more than $10 million in 1999 to turn *The American Prospect* (TAP) into a slick leftwing monthly journal of opinion. TAP's editor-at-large Harold Meyerson is vice-chair of Democratic Socialists of America. Other TAP writers include co-founders Robert Kuttner, the economics pundit, and former Clinton Labor Secretary Robert Reich.

Major 2003 grants include $4 million to the Florence Fund (executive director, John Moyers, Bill's son), which sponsors of TomPaine.com, an online magazine that funds anti-war ads and reports; $1.5 million to the Public Citizen Foundation; and $277,000 to Link Media to fund *Salon* magazine investigative journalism.

The list of funding sources for the radical anti-war left could go on, but the point is clear: the movement is well-heeled with millions of dollars. The major foundations, as front-pagemagazine.com writer Ben Johnson has noted, "are only a selective representation of the enormous grant-making power the Left has accrued by capturing the leadership of the nation's largest foundations." Conservatives and those who support a vigorous defense program have no similar funding. A study by the Center for Security Policy in 2000 demonstrated that the ratio in financial power of the Left over the Right is about 10-1 ($40 billion to $4 billion). This is an advantage that, over time, may prove dangerous for our country's future.

The "Intellectuals"

Any assessment of the resources available to anti-war organizers must include the contribution of "intellectuals." Intellectuals provide the rhetoric, the moral arguments and the scholarly prestige to buttress the movement's street chants and placard slogans.

The current intellectual critique of modern American foreign policy is not pacifist or isolationist. It is dominated by neo-Marxists and it originates in the American university. A University of Wisconsin historian, William Appleman Williams, provided the prototypical leftist analysis of U.S. foreign policy in his seminal 1959 work, *The Tragedy of American Diplomacy*. The tragedy? An emerging capitalist elite had constructed a network of connections with the America's political elite after the Civil War and foisted on the public foreign policies that served its own selfish interests. Williams, who attended the Naval Academy and saw service in the Pacific theater, dismissed the political and ethical reasons given for U.S. foreign policies as masks behind which a rising corporate aristocracy skillfully conspired against the people. Williams' book opened the Pandora's box of economic interpretation that remains central to the arguments of today's antiwar protesters. The sloganeering against "Halliburton" can trace its pedigree to Williams.

According to Williams, American capitalism relentlessly pursued overseas markets to offset "the threat of economic stagnation and the fear of social upheaval" at home. Foreign markets would supply the raw materials for home industries while absorbing a burgeoning surplus from America's farms and factories. This ingenious strategy to control foreign markets ("a brilliant strategic stroke") was promoted under the subterfuge of "free trade." "America's overwhelming economic power would cast the economy and the politics of the weaker, underdeveloped countries in a pro-American mold."

Williams' sweeping condemnation of U.S. foreign policy was popular in the academy and was quickly adopted by other writers. For instance, in *Power and Impotence: The Failure of American Foreign Policy* (1966), Edmund Stillman and William Pfaff looked at U.S. policies during the early years of the Cold War. The authors claimed that the policy of containing Communism in Europe after World War II was "a contest for the control of a prostrate but fundamentally very rich continent that had functioned as the center of world politics for three hundred years." Similarly, the neo-Marxist critic Michael Harrington called upon American policymakers to help usher in a new socialist world order. Harrington, the author of *The Other America* (1962), an analysis of poverty that helped inspire President Lyndon Johnson's "Great Society" programs, urged the U.S. to:

institute extensive economic planning and to ignore the allocation of resources made by the market. This clearly has anti-capitalist and social- ist implications... for our time demands a new type of revolution. This means discarding a central assumption of U.S. policy from Harry Truman to the present - that a sophisticated and liberalized free enterprise could provide the economic basis for political democracy in the Third World.

Other social theorists, such as the economist Robert Heilbroner, went so far as to endorse the necessity of worldwide communist revolutionary movements in support of "a philosophy that approves authoritarian and collectivist measures at home and that utilizes as the target for its national resentment abroad the towering villains of the world, of which the United States is now Number One." Writing in 1966, Heilbroner specified the "most applicable" areas for revolution—"the crowded land masses and archipelagoes of Southeast Asia and the impoverished areas of Central and South America." Heilbroner's wish came true. American foreign policy focused on precisely those areas for the next two decades.

The American college campus has been a center for leftist anti-war activity. Neo-Communist leftists of various stripes are embedded in the faculties of America's elite universities; in some cases the most prominent leftists of the Vietnam War era are still on campus.

Much higher education no longer seeks the disinterested

pursuit of knowledge or what used to be called "the truth." Instead it promotes an overt political agenda and it treats the classroom as a political battleground for attacking "racism," "sexism" and "capitalism." In the humanities and social sciences and in campus "peace studies" programs American institutions and policies, including U.S. foreign policy, international relations, and the causes of war, are explained in terms of race, class, and gender. The goal is activism, not inquiry. Radicalized professors expect college campuses to be frontlines in an ideological war against society.

Years ago, addressing at an annual meeting of the American Studies Association, the historian John Patrick Diggins described how college campuses had changed. "When my generation of liberals was in control of university faculties in the Sixties," Diggins said, "we opened the doors to the hiring of radicals in the name of diversity. We thought you would do the same. But you didn't. You closed the doors behind you."

University of Virginia philosophy professor Richard Rorty, editor of the socialist journal *Dissent* and a leading "public intellectual," has described this transformation:

The power base of the left in America is now in the universities, since the trade unions have largely been killed off. The universities have done a lot of good work by setting up, for example, African-American studies programs, Women's Studies programs, Gay and Lesbian programs. They have created power bases for these movements.

Who are the intellectual apostles of this movement? A key figure is a little-known Italian Communist who spent much of his adult life in prison.

Antonio Gramsci

The ideological theory for the new role for the American university goes back to the 1930's and an Italian Marxist named Antonio Gramsci. Gramsci wondered why Italian workers supported Mussolini's black-shirted Fascists instead of the Communist party during the Depression. Had not Marx explained that desperately poor workers would seize the "means of production" and create a revolution? What had gone wrong?

Gramsci concluded that Marx rightly understood the importance of "class struggle" but had focused on the wrong class.

Marx was mistaken when he argued that the working class must be the instrument of capitalism's destruction. Culture, not the economy, was what mattered in modern society; and that meant the agents of social change were intellectuals, not workers. Gramsci urged the revolution to seize the means of *intellectual* production. That meant winning control of the university system and the mass media. Gramsci argued that revolutionary intellectuals would need to capture what he called the "cultural hegemony" of society.

In a series of notes he made during his long incarceration (he was one of Mussolini's political prisoners), Gramsci updated Marxist theory by explaining that society would be transformed by intellectuals—the idea producers—establishing cultural hegemony over Western society. Gramsci's hegemony is what the radicalized academic elite has in mind for the U.S. According to Gramsci:

> Critical self-consciousness means historically and politically, the creation of an elite of intellectuals. A human mass does not distinguish itself, does not become independent in its own right without, in the widest sense, organizing itself, and there is no organization without intellectuals, that is without organisers and leaders... But the process of creating intellectuals is long and difficult, full of contradictions, advances and retreats, dispersal and regrouping, in which the loyalty of the masses is often sorely tried.

American Marxist intellectuals latched on to Gramsci's theory of how to change society. The baby-boom post-Vietnam generation, they said, had grown up on a steady diet of movies and television. Modern popular culture was the product of mass media indoctrination pumped into the classroom, the shopping mall, and the living room.

No communist conspiracy was necessary to capture the public's idle mind. Instead, a complacent "mass public" could be made to accept politically correct ideas by an intellectual elite that succeeded in dominating the campus, the press, churches, Hollywood and other arbiters of conventional thinking.

According to the Gramsci-influenced sociologist Dominic Strinati:

Pop culture and the mass media are subject to the production, reproduction and transformation of hegemony through the institution of civil society, which cover the areas of cultural production and consumption. Hegemony operates culturally and ideologically through the institutions of civil society which characterize mature liberal-democratic, capitalist societies. These institutions include education, the family, the church, the mass media, popular culture etc.

Many Leftist intellectuals who support the antiwar movement endorse Gramsci's theory of "cultural hegemony." They are not interested in stirring up the working class or inflaming "the masses." Instead, they want to incorporate anti-capitalist, radical feminist, and extreme racialist and gender ideologies into their writing and teaching, and then use them to influence the wider culture. Noam Chomsky leads this pack, but there are others who provide the reasons and arguments to justify anti-war activism.

Here are representative sketches of some of the principal intellectuals of the modern Left:

Noam Chomsky. A prime example: Dr. Noam Chomsky, professor of linguistics at MIT since 1955. Chomsky, now 75, remains the most conspicuous American intellectual to rationalize the Al Qaeda attacks of 9/11.

In his 2003 book *Power and Terror* Chomsky downplays the American loss of life on 9/11 by comparing it to the "far more extreme terrorism" of U.S. foreign policy:

There's a famous definition in the Gospels of the hypocrite, and a hypocrite is the person who refuses to apply to himself the standards he applies to others. By that standard, the entire commentary and discussion of the so-called War on Terror is pure hypocrisy... without exception.

Once described by the *New York Times* as "arguably the most important intellectual alive," Chomsky has devoted over a half-century to leftist activism and apologetics. He is an admirer of Cambodia's murderous Pol Pot, Mao Tse-tung, Fidel Castro and Ho Chi Minh. He called Viet Cong terror "justified" and defended Mao's China as a "just society"—this shortly after the purges of 1958–1962 killed an estimated 30 million Chinese. By comparison he labels American democracy a "four year dictatorship" and suggests that the U.S. needs "a kind of denazification." "By any objective standard," he wrote, "the United States has become the most aggressive power in the world, the greatest threat to peace, to national self-determination, and to international cooperation."

Chomsky is no profound theorist; his voluminous political writing is utopian and directed to a general audience (which may explain its appeal to students). He claims to be an anti-Bolshevist and to support what he calls "libertarian socialism," which he ascribes to the nineteenth century anarchist Mikhail Bakunin. His model society: the anarchists of Barcelona during the Spanish Civil War.

Chomsky's star has lately been glowing brighter than ever. Since 9/11 he's had two best-selling books. *Power and Terror* even became a documentary movie. His nationwide lecture tours generate loads of publicity. At the University of California Chomsky gave five days of political talks to an estimated 5,000 students. A press profile, "Conscience of a Nation," in *The Guardian,* a British daily, compared his significance to Marx, Shakespeare and the Bible. Overstatement? Maybe not, considering the generations of students who have taken to the streets after reading Noam Chomsky's anti-American screeds.

Many other prominent academics speak and write against war and imperialism, leading naïve outsiders to mistake them for campus gadflies. But it's important to understand that the academic Left organizes systemic, ideological dissent. Its disagreement is not over a policy—the invasion of Iraq—or the tactics used in the war on terror. Chomsky and his counterparts oppose the principles that define America and regard its institutions as debased and corrupt. A reformer would propose changes to law and policy, but would-be revolutionaries want to destroy the social order.

Gabriel Kolko. Like Chomsky, Kolko is a radical and socialist who blends Marxism-Stalinism into his own interpretation of American life and culture. A Harvard graduate, Kolko has spent most of his life on the faculty of York University in Toronto, where he has authored ten books on U.S. history and foreign policy, including two on the Cold War, two on Vietnam, and an analysis of the causes of 9/11. Kolko more than Chomsky is the role model for "New Left" historians; his books are used as texts at major universities, and they are praised by mainstream reviewers even though an almost paranoid anti-American tone runs through their content.

Kolko has called the United States "intellectually and culturally undeveloped," "blind to itself—its past, its present, and its future," an "evil society." In *The Politics of War* (1968), he argued that the United States was responsible for the Cold War and praised Stalin as a pragmatic defender of Russian interests who displayed "flexibility and subtlety" in his foreign policy. In *Anatomy of a War: Vietnam, the United States and the Modern Historical Experience* (1994), Kolko effusively described Ho Chi Minh and his Communist colleagues as "collegial" and "cooperative... free of the problems of egoism." Though they killed millions of Vietnamese Kolko portrays them as benevolent leaders who insisted that "nothing could be done to hurt their property." In *Vietnam: Anatomy of a Peace* (1997) Kolko argues that the Communists won the war but lost the peace after 1975. He worries that military victory eroded Vietnam's socialism and let in free markets. He even criticizes Vietnam's leaders after Ho for developing economic policies in the late 1980's that were "based on a crude historical fiction, which conservative Chicago-school theorists and Reagan Republicans also share, that exculpates the corruption and social disorientation and disillusion it nominally deplores."

Kolko's popularity in the academy should not be surprising. Many faculty do not dismiss his starting point—that the U.S. is a totalitarian society—as an outrage, but regard it as an arguable point. Kolko is a typically abrasive public intellectual who attacks the social order that gives him the freedom denied in the societies he praises. He denounces a "ruling class" because it has made America a free country, or, as he puts it: "defines the preconditions and functions of the larger American social order, with its security and continuity as an institution being the political order's central goal in the post-Civil War historical experience." Similarly, Kolko interprets U.S. foreign policy as an effort to "restructure the world so that American business could trade, operate and profit without restrictions everywhere."

During the Vietnam War Kolko traveled to Hanoi, met with Communist officials and advised them on the best way to defeat the U.S. He has praised Stalinist dictatorships that enslaved and killed millions of their own people. Mao Tse-tung, he writes, is guided by "honesty, efficiency and moderation." North Korea's Kim Il-sung was a "national hero" whose social reforms included "a massive education program ...extensive worker welfare decrees regulating working hours, vacations and social insurance."

Since September 11, 2001 Kolko has been a prolific writer. In *Another Century of War?* (2002) and in articles for the radical *Counterpunch* magazine, Kolko condemns the American response to al Qaeda as imperialistic and unjust. "Suffice it to say," he concludes, "that the United States' sponsorship ... of state terrorism is one of the crucial reasons it now has to confront violence on its own soil. History has come full circle."

Howard Zinn. This retired Boston University professor commands wide popular attention even though he is a committed and doctrinaire Marxist. Howard Zinn is the author of over twenty books and plays, including the popular *People's History of the United States.*

An activist as much as a historian, Zinn disdains traditional scholarship. His *People's History* is an unapologetic Marxist interpretation of American history that contains no source citations. Zinn is "not troubled by that," because, "the mountain of books under which we all stand leans so heavily in the other direction—so tremblingly respectful of states and statesmen and so disrespectful, by inattention, to people's movements—that we need some counterforce to avoid being crushed into submission."

Zinn seems to believe telling a story makes it so. History thus becomes action, and historians and their students become activists. The classroom is a Leninist political cell. "I wanted my writing of history and my teaching of history to be part of a social struggle," Zinn has confessed, "I wanted to be part of history and not just a recorder and teacher of history. So that kind of attitude towards history, history itself as a political act, has always informed my writing and my teaching."

A *People's History* has sold over one million copies. (First published in 1980, the revised edition of the *People's History* recently ranked number 92 in Amazon.com sales.) If students believe George Washington was the richest man in America and that 1776 was all about profit and greed, then they probably have read Howard Zinn. If they believe the U.S. is made up of oppressed and oppressor classes, that the Puritans were racists, and that Pearl Harbor and the Cold War are America's fault, they probably have read Howard Zinn. And if they think Saddam Hussein is a victim of "that macho feeling that people in power have about the United States being the number one superpower and determined to show it" (as Zinn told Bill Moyers on PBS), then we know the source of their belief. "Knowledge is Power" is a famous dictum. History by leftists reminds us that ignorance is powerful too.

Herbert Aptheker. Although he died at age 87 in 2003, in his time Herbert Aptheker was labeled the "chief theoretician" of the Communist Party, USA. He should be counted as one of the top anti-war activists in modern American history, especially during the Vietnam era. Although he is gone, Aptheker's legacy remains both a symbol of the movement in its heyday and a reminder of the tactical and theoretical substance still underpinning anti-war activism.

In 1966 Aptheker provided the then-nascent anti-war movement with a propaganda boost when he, along with historian Staughton Lynd and SDS leader Tom Hayden, traveled to Hanoi for what they claimed was an attempt to "sound out" the North Vietnamese on the possibility of a peace settlement. In fact, their trip was a strategic mission to tie the fortunes of the American peace movement to Hanoi's prosecution of the war. What seemed a brilliant alliance from the anti-war perspective enraged patriotic Americans. But the pilgrimage served the protest movement's own *un*-patriotic cause.

As America's leading Stalinist intellectual, Aptheker paved the way for the shrill rhetoric and theories of leftist academics who won tenure after Vietnam. Throughout his life, Aptheker denounced his country's leaders in the harshest of terms. They were a totalitarian corporate elite "so putrid… that it no longer dares to permit its people to live at all." They had "the morals of goats, the learning of gorillas and the ethics of racist, war-inciting enemies of humanity, rotten to the core, parasitic, merciless and doomed."

Despite the many crimes of the Stalin era, Aptheker refused to denounce Stalin, once describing the gulag-ridden and destitute USSR as a country standing tall for "socialism, national liberation, equality and peace." He was one of a few American Communists to defend the 1956 Soviet occupation of Hungary, describing it in *The Truth About Hungary* as a necessary defense against a potential U.S.-led coup.

Despite such absurdities, Aptheker received respectful recognition from the liberal media. The *New York Times* obituary called him an "outspoken" defender of civil rights and "one of the first scholars to denounce American military involvement in Vietnam." Aptheker was hardly a scholar; after the publication of *American Negro Slave Revolts,* his revised 1943 dissertation, the Communist Party tightly censored Aptheker's subsequent works.

Eric Foner. This Columbia University historian called Aptheker's work on American blacks "a landmark in Afro-American history." Foner is no fringe academic. He is a former president of both the American Historical Association and the Organization of American Historians. An established scholar of nineteenth century American history, he has published award-winning books on the politics of the Civil War era and Reconstruction.

He is also a political leftist; his uncle, the labor historian Philip Foner, and father were Communist party members. Foner has defended the Rosenbergs, Paul Robeson, Angela Davis and other Communists. "An unabashed apologist for the Soviet system and an unforgiving historian of America," according to historian John Diggins, Foner's politics has done nothing to dampen his stellar academic career.

After the 9/11 attacks Foner equated the terrorists with the Bush Administration in an article written for the *London Review of Books.* "I'm not sure which is more frightening," he wrote, "the horror that engulfed New York City or the apocalyptic rhetoric emanating from the White House." At rallies and in Vietnam era-style "teach-ins" Foner defended his attacks on U.S. policy as a form of patriotism: "I refuse to cede the definition of American patriotism to George W. Bush. I have a different definition of patriotism, which comes from Paul Robeson: The patriot is the person who is never satisfied with his country." Robeson, an African-American singer/actor and Communist, was so satisfied with the Soviet Union that he accepted the 1952 Stalin Peace Prize.

Foner mixes his professional and political lives. He and long-time Communist Party member David Montgomery, another past president of the Organization of American Historians (OAH), formed a caucus at the OAH annual meeting in 2003 called Historians Against the War. Its stated purpose is "to investigate reports of repressive measures having an impact upon historians' teaching, research, employment and freedom of expression."

In fact, Historians Against War puts professional historians on record as political opponents of the U.S. government. In 2003 the group became a member organization of the United for Peace and Justice (UPJ) coalition and joined the October 25, 2003 march in Washington that UPJ co-sponsored with ANSWER. In 2004 at the OAH annual meeting in Boston Historians Against War sponsored a petition signed by 1300 historians berating the Bush Administration for its response to the terror attacks. The petition, in part, reads:

> As historians, teachers and scholars, we oppose the expansion of the United States empire and the doctrine of pre-emptive war that have led to the occupation of Iraq. We deplore the secrecy, deception and distortion of history involved in the administration's conduct of a war that violates international law, intensifies attacks on civil liberties and reaches toward domination of the Middle East and its resources.

Barbara Kingsolver. Kingsolver is the author of nine best-selling novels, story collections and non-fiction books over the past fifteen years, including the highly praised *The Poisonwood Bible* (1998) and *Prodigal Summer* (2001). Unfortunately, her literary talents do not carry over into political judgment, as Kingsolver plays her part in the intellectual assault on the war against terror. Her poison pen is directed at President Bush and the culture she thinks he represents. She is becoming a literary Michael Moore.

In her many op-ed pieces before and since 9/11 Kingsolver vilifies the U.S. with rhetoric. The U.S., she has charged, is the world's "fat brother," responsible for a "prideful wastefulness

[and] a noisy celebratory appetite for unnecessary things." Even before the terrorist attacks, she endorsed the anti-globalization crowd that now provides street fighters for the anti-war movement. The Bush Administration's refusal to ratify the Kyoto Accords left her "stunned" by the "selfishness of that act."

Kingsolver's reactions to the terror attacks fit the same mold. In one Los Angles Times op-ed published one month after 9/11 she announced her opposition to attacking the Taliban in Afghanistan. Entitled "No Glory in Unjust War on the Weak," she draws anti-war conclusions from her fears:

> I cannot find the glory in this day. When I picked up the newspaper and saw, 'America Strikes Back!' blazed across it in letters I swear were 10 inches tall—shouldn't they reserve at least one type size for something like, say, nuclear war?—my heart sank. We've answered one terrorist attack with another, raining death on the most war-scarred, terrified populace that ever crept to a doorway and looked out.
>
> ...adversaries simply say I am ridiculous, a dreamer who takes a child's view of the world, imagining it can be made better than it is. The more sophisticated approach, they suggest, is to accept that we are all on a jolly road trip down the maw of catastrophe, so shut up and drive. I fight that, I fight that as if I'm drowning.

Beautiful prose, heartfelt thoughts that serve the terrorists' cause.

Tariq Ramadan. One prominent academic center recently achieved notoriety when it invited an advocate of *jihad* to join its peace studies faculty. Until the Department of Homeland Security rescinded his visa a professor named Tariq Ramadan was scheduled to be the Henry Luce professor at the Joan B. Kroc Institute for International Peace Studies at Notre Dame University. (*Jihad* is the Arabic word for "holy war." By contrast, Kroc was the late wife of the founder of McDonald's; Luce was the publisher of *Time* magazine and the great champion of the "American Century"; Notre Dame is a Catholic university in Indiana.)

Most Americans will not recognize his name, but Tariq Ramadan may well be the most dangerous anti-American intellectual in the world. Ramadan is a 42 year-old, Swiss-born

73

multimillionaire leader of the worldwide Islamic rebellion against the West. The author of 12 books and 170 audiotapes on the Islamic revival movement, Ramadan is a tireless globe-trotter who has issued a clarion call among Muslims for an international *jihad*. Arnaud De Borchgrave in the *Washington Times* writes that Ramadan is "lionized by the jobless, North African slum-dwellers that cling barnaclelike to France's major cities. The neo-Marxist anti-globalization left has also hitched its bandwagon to his star-status in French-speaking Europe."

As the grandson of the founder of the Muslim Brotherhood, the most important Islamist movement of the last century, Ramadan has become the leading anti-American and anti-Semitic theoretician in Europe for the vast Arab world. A spellbinding speaker and prolific author, he has won over many academic liberals with guile and charm.

But Ramadan offers an apocalyptic vision of a new world order, which he says will realize the final destruction of the West: "The West will begin its new decline, and the Arab-Islamic world its renewal." His major work, *To Be a European Muslim* (1999) is printed in fourteen languages and makes no apologies for declaring war on western capitalist society:

> Only Islam can achieve the synthesis between Christianity and humanism, and fill the spiritual void that afflicts the West... Today the Muslims who live in the West must unite themselves to the revolution of the anti-establishment groups from the moment when the neoliberal capitalist system becomes, for Islam, a theater of war.

Famous in Europe, Ramadan has become a popular lecturer at U.S. universities. Lenin is said to have remarked that the bourgeois West would sell him the rope he would use to hang it. Apparently, Notre Dame was about to do just that with Tariq Ramadan when the federal government denied him entry into the U.S.

Chapter 3

AMERICA'S "MANIFEST DESTINY" AND THE PEACE MOVEMENT

To criticize the current anti-war movement is not to attack all anti-war dissent. Questioning authority, dissenting opinion and active protest are important parts of the American heritage. Is anti-war dissent exceptional to America or a characteristic of all healthy democracies? It's hard to say. It is clear, however, that for over three centuries the anti-war impulse has been a central part of America's democratic society. The nation's record of anti-war resistance and peace reform has no equal, not even in Great Britain.

Historian Charles DeBeneditti has studied American peace activists and has identified certain characteristics common to them: First, peace activists see war as unacceptable. They regard it as destructive to society, humanity and Christian values. Second, activists looked for alternative ways to resolve conflict, promote harmony, and create social change. Some find an answer in models of utopian community. Others resort to progressive reform politics.

In the twentieth century, however, another dimension has been added to this profile. For many modern activists "peace" is a deceptive tool of ideological warfare. Peace is not a valued end in itself but a tactical argument that activists use to achieve other ends—the overturn of capitalism, racism, sexism and other allegations of "oppression." As the previous chapters indicate, left-wing anti-war activists use peace as a pretext for radical politics.

75

The deceptive appeal for peace has a long history: it was an essential part of the strategy of subversion used by the Bolsheviks during the Russian Revolution. In the 1920's and 30's the Comintern promoted front groups that advocated peace activism; so did the Soviet Union during the first years of the Cold War. Surprisingly, more than a decade after the demise of Soviet Communism, Communist front groups still dominate the American peace movement.

Nonetheless, it's important to recall the earlier peace activism in American history that is untainted by leftist ideology. There is a cultural wellspring of war resistance in America's past. It includes pacifists and presidents, isolationists and internationalists, socialists and libertarians, wild-eyed utopians and calculating business tycoons.

Communities of Peace

In the American colonies the peace movement had its roots in Europe and, like almost everything else, was steeped in religion. The Puritans were ambivalent about war and peace: they believed in fighting to defend religious faith, but their exodus to the New World stemmed from a desire to be free of Europe's sectarian struggles, and they attempted to build in the Massachusetts Bay Colony a model biblical community of harmony and peace. The "Wilsonian" streak in modern American foreign and military policies undoubtedly owes much to the seventeenth century Puritans, who formed communities of peace but went armed on spiritual patrol.

The same tension appears in the eighteenth century Quakers. William Penn created a colony for those who followed the "inner light." His model Christian community, framed in 1682, was marked by social consensus, representative government and religious toleration. Quakers opposed oath-taking, militia drilling, jury service, taxation and warfare. Pennsylvania also became home to Mennonites, the Church of the Brethren ("Dunkers"), Anabaptists and the Amish, who created Church-centered pockets of pacifist resistance to secular authority.

Yet pacifism ran head-on against political and military

necessities. In 1755 the Pennsylvania Assembly supported a war tax at the start of the French and Indian War. It split Quaker unity and forced the resignation of many members of the Society of Friends from the Assembly. The conflict between conscience and nation intensified during the War of Independence. A Quaker mother probably inspired Thomas Paine, who argued in *The Rights of Man* that the rights of the governed are derived from popular consent and not state power. Why should the colonies pay for Britain's wars? No social purpose, wrote Paine in *The Age of Reason,* could be found for war. Reason, not force, should resolve disputes among men and nations.

The New World celebrated peace; war was the province of "old Europe." In 1793 Dr. Benjamin Rush proposed a Peace Office and a Secretary of Peace who would be "free from all the present absurd and vulgar European prejudices upon the subject of government; let him be a genuine republican and a sincere Christian." Three years later President Washington admonished his countrymen to stay out of Europe's quarrels. Most policymakers for the next century took careful heed of Washington's "Farewell Address."

The first civic association dedicated to peace was the American Peace Society (APS), formed in 1828 to promote negotiation, arbitration and the eventual settlement of disputes by a Congress of Christian Nations "enlightened by the rays of the gospel of peace." The peace movement was associated with the other great reform movements of the mid-nineteenth century, including prison reform, temperance, feminism and abolition. Indeed, so many women were recruited to the peace cause that men equated peace with them. "Men make war," wrote the Society's William Ladd in an 1836 pamphlet, *On the Duties of Females to Promote Peace.* "Let women make peace."

The American Peace Society advocated the abolition of slavery. Eventually, Northern opinion would associate abolition with peace and slavery with aggression and war. In that sense, the peace movement aggravated the growing national schism. When the war came, peace supporters rallied to the Union. However, that meant slavery's abolition replaced peace as the ultimate good, an ironic position for a peace movement.

Northerners who opposed war, the so-called "copperheads," opened up one of the great contradictions of the history of U.S.

anti-war activism. They called President Lincoln a "dictator" and interfered with enlistments in the Union Army. Many were members of Congress, which made their opposition to the war all the more visible. Secretary of War Edwin Stanton decreed that anyone "engaged by act, speech, or writing, in discouraging volunteer enlistments, or in any way giving aid and comfort to the enemy, or in any other disloyal practice against the United States" would be subject to arrest and trial "before a military commission." Lincoln suspended habeas corpus and over 13,000 war opponents were eventually arrested, held without civil trial and prosecuted by military tribunals. Had these "Peace Democrats" prevailed there would be no United States of America.

The arguments against war and imperialism that roiled the latter half of the nineteenth and early twentieth centuries—over U.S. occupation of Hawaii, the Philippines and countries in the Caribbean from Haiti to Panama—in many respects repeat a debate that had begun during America's 1846-1848 war with Mexico. When President Polk dispatched General Zachary Taylor and 1500 men to cross the Rio Grande, prompting a Mexican attack, he justified his war message by arguing that the U.S. was attacked on its own territory. This provoked a certain congressman, Abraham Lincoln of Illinois, to demand the evidence of the exact "spot" on American soil where the attack took place. "War hawks" of the time called him "spotty" Lincoln, but the point was not lost on his contemporaries.

Ulysses S. Grant, arguably the nineteenth century's most violent warrior, was Lincoln's kindred spirit well before the Civil War. In 1847, Grant fought in Mexico as a young lieutenant fresh out of West Point. But in his celebrated *Memoirs*, completed just before his death in 1885, Grant labeled the Mexican War "the most unjust war ever waged by a stronger against a weaker nation... an instance of a republic following the bad example of European monarchies."

It is one of those ironies of history that Abraham Lincoln and Ulysses S. Grant, the civil and military leaders who prosecuted a "total war" against secession, were forceful opponents of the war with Mexico. That should give pause to anyone who too quickly condemns antiwar "agitators."

Expansionism: The Political Costs of Small Wars

America's first terrorist attack occurred on August 24-25, 1814, when the British Army attacked Washington, D.C. and burned down the Capitol and the White House. The U.S. diplomatic response came in due time. Initially, this took the form of the Monroe Doctrine, issued "unilaterally" in 1823 as an assertion that Latin America was a closed political system to outside authority. The Monroe Doctrine formally announced, "We should consider any attempt on their [European] part to extend their system to any portion of this hemisphere as dangerous to our peace and safety." Monroe's initial intent was to preserve the newly-won freedoms of the area against potential Spanish and other interventions. But the Doctrine soon took on a life of its own and provided cover for a series of "pre-emptive" U.S. incursions under the banner of national security and visions of "Manifest Destiny."

This period of our national history is properly called the era of "expansionism." From Monroe to Polk, McKinley and Theodore Roosevelt, American presidents responded to foreign disturbances with a sustained campaign of what later observers would call "unilateralism" and "pre-emption." American presidents forbade foreign powers from intervening in hemispheric affairs or exercising a strategic influence contrary to U.S. interests. It was a time of authentic U.S. "hegemony." By 1898, after the War with Spain and the occupation of the Philippines, the U.S. extended its "sphere of influence" into Caribbean and mid-Pacific waters.

The era witnessed a series of "small wars"—overseas American interventions and occupations to put down insurrections and guerrilla campaigns. These U.S. actions abroad sometimes produced an anti-war backlash at home, one that bears comparison to the anti-war protest against U.S. military involvement in Iraq today or in Vietnam forty years ago. We tend to forget the protest movements of over a century ago because they do not celebrate American military victories and were generally unruly, anti-establishment and unpopular. Still, they are haunting memories of the domestic political costs of U.S. foreign occupation.

Peace movements cannot be evaluated apart from their

strategic setting. The Monroe Doctrine, for instance, represented a defensive U.S. foreign policy during a period when the U.S. actually had no power to enforce what was an explosive document on paper, one that asserted a U.S. intention to keep the entire hemisphere free from outside influence.

But after the Civil War settled the question of national unity the U.S. began to look beyond its own borders. It not only proclaimed an American sphere of influence in the Western hemisphere, it acted on its proclamations.

By the end of the century the U.S. was a vast industrial and commercial powerhouse that had set its sights on nothing less than imperial dominion over areas within its reach. Expansion became a national ideology and would continue to guide U.S. national interests until Franklin D. Roosevelt adopted the Good Neighbor Policy in 1933. During this time Americans would land military forces on Caribbean islands and in lands in the Far East on more than twenty-five occasions.

The American peace movement opposed these foreign military occupations. A look at its response to the U.S. military occupation of the Philippines and Nicaragua offers our own time some important lessons.

Manifest Destiny

After the American Founding, what was called the "expansion movement" picked up increasing geopolitical and ideological momentum. Americans came to regard expansion as inevitable and fundamental to the national identity. To Americans, expansion was no land grab; it was divinely sponsored and "manifest" by nature, less a series of calculated decisions than a human spontaneous combustion.

This is apparent in President McKinley's instructions to the American peace commissioners who were drafting the treaty to end the Spanish-American War and annex the Philippines. McKinley dictated a thesis of "inevitability":

Without any original thought of complete or even partial acquisition, the presence and success of our arms at Manila imposes

80

upon us obligations which we cannot disregard. The march of events rules and overrules human action.

This idea was hardly original to McKinley. In 1845 a journalist-publicist named John O'Sullivan identified America's "Manifest Destiny," which was nothing less than divinely-inspired: "Our manifest destiny [is] to overspread the continent allotted by Providence for the free development of our yearly developing millions." America's goals were not a calculated exploration for New World riches or an Old World conquest for power and colonies. Unlike many of Europe's imperialists, Americans were sincere when they claimed to be pursuing a civilizing mission abroad.

Of course, expansion also reflected fear and the need for self-defense. "Pre-emptive war" was very much on the minds of Americans who kept a watchful eye on an aggressive France in control of Louisiana and a Great Britain still in possession of large portions of the North American continent. George Washington himself observed in 1799 that "Offensive operations often times is the surest, if not the only means of defence." America's national security required a westward movement to preemptively secure the frontier.

By the end of the nineteenth century, with the nation's natural boundaries fixed at the Rio Grande, the Canadian border and the Pacific Ocean, the expansion movement went overseas. The defensive concept of the Monroe Doctrine changed shape; the shield became a sword.

Elihu Root, Theodore Roosevelt's Secretary of State, held a pre-emptive interpretation of the Monroe Doctrine, on one occasion proclaiming that it was "the right of every sovereign state to protect itself by preventing a condition in which it will be too late to protect itself." Wilson's Secretary of State Robert Lansing demonstrated the same mindset in his diplomacy. Lansing wanted to buy the West Indies from Denmark in 1916 and warned that the U.S. would not hesitate to seize them should it anticipate future trouble with Germany. In his note to the Danish Ambassador, Lansing gave Denmark an offer it couldn't refuse:

In the event of an evident intention on the part of Germany to take possession of his country or to compel Denmark to cede the islands to her, the United States would be under the necessity of seizing and annexing them, and, though it would be done with the greatest reluctance, it would be necessary to do it in order to avoid a serious dispute with the German Government over the sovereignty of and title to the islands, as we would never permit the group to become German.

Denmark sold the islands. Thus, a policy of national self-defense required a doctrine of pre-emptive action: the U.S. announced that it would prevent a potential injury coming from a potential consequence of the potential action of a potential enemy. To anti-expansionists (as well as the Danish ambassador) this policy may have seemed a *reductio ad absurdum,* but to Washington it was a national security priority.

Indeed, for many Americans national expansion required no defense or appeal to national security. John O'Sullivan's rhetoric admitted no limits to expansion:

The far-reaching, the boundless future will be an era of American greatness. In its magnificent domain of space and time, the nation of many nations is destined to manifest to mankind the excellence of divine principles; to establish on earth the noblest temple ever dedicated to the worship of the Most High—the Sacred and the True. Its floor shall be a hemisphere—its roof the firmament of the star-studded heavens, and its congregation a Union of many Republics, comprising hundreds of happy millions.

If national expansion was inevitable, then opposition to it must be irrational. In delivering the Treaty of Paris to Congress in 1898, President McKinley made the principle of Manifest Destiny explicit:

Not only is the union of the Hawaiian territory to the United States no new scheme, but it is the inevitable consequence of the relation steadfastly maintained with that mid-Pacific domain for three-quarters of a century. Its accomplishment... has been merely a question of time. ...Under such circumstances annexation [of the Philippines] is not a change. It is a consummation.

In 1893, Professor Frederick Jackson Turner presented his famous "frontier thesis." Turner explained that the American character was shaped by contact with an ever-expanding frontier over more than two centuries. The qualities needed to settle the frontier had molded "a composite nationality for the American people;" the frontier was responsible for a continent-wide movement of democracy, materialism, individualism and practicality. But hunters and trappers had given way to farms and towns, which were now being replaced by cities and industries. Turner wondered whether the end of the frontier meant an end to the American character.

Turner feared the end of an old frontier, but the expansionists of 1898 celebrated the beginnings of a new one. At the end of the century the U.S. was exploring an overseas frontier in the islands of the Caribbean, the Central American isthmus and the Philippine Islands in the distant Pacific. America's "imperial era" had begun.

The new era of westward expansion was celebrated by supporters of a new U.S. Navy, particularly Alfred Thayer Mahan, the great apostle of seapower whose book *The Influence of Seapower Upon History* was published in 1890. A new two-ocean, battleship-heavy navy replaced the railroad as the engine of American expansion.

The literary expression of expansion can be found in the writings and speeches of Theodore Roosevelt, as the following passage (one among hundreds) attests:

Barbarism has, and can have, no place in a civilized world. It is our duty toward the people living in barbarism to see that they are freed from their chains, and we can free them only by destroying barbarism itself. The missionary, the merchant, and the soldier may each have a part to play in this destruction, and in the consequent uplifting of the people.

Expansion was "liberating," "inevitable," and "necessary" for self-defense. Senator Orville Platt (R-CT) was author of the Amendment bearing his name that placed Cuban independence under a virtual American protectorate. He held that annexation of the Philippines would be "in accordance with the irresistible law of growth."

President McKinley's war message against Spain in April 1898 was welcomed by the public and Congress. On May 1, 1898 Admiral Dewey blasted the Spanish navy from Manila Bay. McKinley sought divine inspiration and declared for annexation (although he confessed he could not locate the Philippines on a map within 2,000 miles). In August the American Army began arriving in the islands, and in December the Treaty of Paris surrendered Spain's authority to the United States. The conquest of Cuba and the Philippines had taken little more than three months.

However, in the Philippines the U.S. Army faced a new era of military pacification that would take more than three years. The "real" war with Spain was abrupt and short; but the war against the Philippine "insurrectos" that followed was long, costly and divisive. The United States stumbled into an overseas military occupation that gave rise to America's first organized anti-war movement.

The Philippine Insurrection

Just before the war with Spain Americans who were interested in peace tended to promote such abstract ideas as disarmament and a world court. The Christian Social Gospel movement, the Salvation Army, and the industrialist Andrew Carnegie supported arbitration agreements, which in theory served as models for sustaining world peace. One new organization, the Universal Peace Union, urged American society to restructure itself along Christian lines. Its leader, appropriately named Alfred Love, led pro-peace summer festivals in the 1890s in the appropriately named village of Mystic, Connecticut. Love's carnivals featured theater, games, peace displays and the climactic release of hundreds of white doves. "Peace and Love" were literal symbols of anti-war activism.

Americans also discovered Russian writer Leo Tolstoy who preached a form of Christian anarchism. He believed love and humanity could combat oppressive state force and private property, the sources of evil. Tolstoy counseled nonviolent resistance to coercive authority. Many Americans were drawn to his teachings, including the Chicago social reformer Jane Addams, William Jennings Bryan and the lawyer Clarence Darrow, Bryan's future courtroom adversary.

In February 1898 the battleship *Maine* exploded in Havana harbor and in April the U.S. declared war on Spain. Peace advocates were divided as abstract moralizing gave way to action. The Mormon Church surrendered its tradition of pacifism and supported President McKinley. But the American Peace Society officially registered its "intense disappointment" with the war; APS leader Benjamin Trueblood predicted that the peace movement would "break forth somewhere in a new tidal wave after the war closes, just as it has done after each of the war periods of the century."

Opponents of American expansionism, who had watched the rising power of the Navy and the taking of Hawaii in 1893, grew more anxious. Then on June 15, 1898, a large crowd of anti-war reformers met at Faneuil Hall in Boston to organize the Anti-Imperialist League. Led by Gamaliel Bradford, a direct descendant of a Mayflower colonist, the movement soon mushroomed to include feminists, social reformers, educators, journalists, lawyers and clergy. Working with other anti-war groups, the Anti-Imperialist League quickly enrolled over 30,000 members.

By 1900 the U.S. was in control of Puerto Rico, Hawaii, Samoa, Guam and the Philippines. The anti-imperialists set their sights on the upcoming presidential election as a great contest to decide the future direction of American foreign policy. They framed the issues: Was the United States a republic or an empire? Could a republic include alien populations? Were "citizens" of a republic different from "subjects" of an empire? To anti-imperialists the central issue was the fundamental nature of American democracy.

After sharp debate the Senate ratified the Treaty of Paris by one vote. But the arguments continued as a guerilla war in the Philippines dragged on. Led by New Englanders, the anti-imperialist cause began to capture more and more popular support even as the rebel leader, Emilio Aguinaldo, espoused the cause of Philippine independence from a mountain hold-out seven thousand miles away.

Anti-war sentiment spread across New England and then crossed the country, according to an eye-witness, "at floodtide." Anti-imperialists organized clubs and societies, and distributed mass quantities of literature. Eminent figures like Andrew Carnegie, Mark Twain and the philosopher William James publicly supported the antiwar cause. By 1900 the Anti-Imperialist League, headquartered in Boston, had over forty branches.

85

The national split was reflected in both political parties and in Congress. The minority Democrats included Anti-Imperialist League officers such as Senators Donelson Caffery of Louisiana and Ben Tillman of South Carolina, while the Republican majority looked to Massachusetts Senator Henry Cabot Lodge and Indiana's Albert Beveridge to defend the cause of expansion. The 1900 Democratic party platform even put imperialism ahead of the currency, William Jennings Bryan's trademark issue.

The anti-imperialist arguments drew upon religion, pacifism and democracy and made appeals to the American character. But anti-imperialists also made other assertions that are eerily familiar today.

They attacked the war as unauthorized by Congress and therefore unconstitutional. Key decision-makers in the Administration, the Republican Party and the military were demonized as conspiring to lead the nation to war. Bryan attacked the millions spent on the war instead of on schools, roads and irrigation projects. The Administration, he said, "would rather waste blood than save water."

Anti-imperalists also claimed a few large corporations were eager for the spoils of victory. This would become a central part of Bryan's presidential campaign against McKinley. Accepting the Democratic nomination Bryan proclaimed:

Imperialism would be profitable to the army contractors; it would be profitable to the shipowners, who would carry live soldiers to the Philippines and bring dead soldiers back; it would be profitable to those who would seize upon the franchise, and it would be profitable to the officials whose salaries would be fixed and paid there; but to the farmer and the laboring man, and to the vast majority of those engaged in other occupations, it would bring expenditures without returns and risk without reward.

Racism also crept into the national debate. Southern politicians like Senators Caffery and Tillman and many northerners were unwilling to accept non-whites, even as colonial subjects. But other anti-imperialists worried that racial discrimination would worsen if America absorbed new populations. Many feared Philippine annexation would lead to more racial exploitation, citing the soldiers' habit of referring to the Filipino as "nigger." Liberals and racists were uncomfortable bedfellows as they opposed the Administration's attempt to put down the insurrection and secure the Philippines as an American colony.

Few anti-imperialists embraced the Philippine insurrection, but there were exceptions. In 1899 Gamaliel Bradford called for an American military defeat "in a moral alliance with the Filipinos." Economist Edward Atkinson published anti-war pamphlets with titles like *The Cost of a National Crime*, which encouraged young men to avoid military duty: "The way has already become plain for the youth of the land to avoid disease and death in the tropics by refusing to volunteer or to enlist in the army or navy of the United States." When Atkinson tried to distribute his work to U.S. troops overseas, the post office pulled his publications from the mail sacks.

Vice President Theodore Roosevelt claimed the anti-imperialists were prolonging the war. And in Manila General Henry Lawton voiced the military's bitterness against the critics of his mission:

If the so-called anti-imperialists...would honestly ascertain the truth on the ground and not in distant America, they would be convinced of the error of their statements and conclusions, and of the unfortunate effect of their publications here. If I am shot by a Filipino bullet it might just as well come from one of my own men, because I know from observations confirmed by captured prisoners that the continuance of fighting is chiefly due to reports that are sent out from America.

A short time later Lawton was felled by a Filipino insurgent.

The war in the Philippines did not go well despite an occupation of 70,000 U.S. soldiers, more than double the original number, and nearly three years of combat. But economic prosperity kept the Republicans in power and the hesitation of many anti-war Republicans to bolt the party undoubtedly hurt the anti-imperialist cause. Despite the anti-war movement, McKinley was re-elected president by a plurality of 7,219,530 to Bryan's 6,351,071.

The Republican victory crushed both the Philippine Insurrection and the anti-war movement. Aguinaldo's guerilla tactics and Bryan's oratory failed to undermine American resolve. By most standards America's subsequent governance of the Philippines was highly successful, and the islands gained their independence in 1946. But Americans may still wonder whether the occupation was worth more than 250,000 civilian Filipino dead and over 4,000 U.S. soldiers killed.

Yale's William Graham Sumner offered an insightful reflection on anti-war dissent in his 1899 essay, "The Conquest of the United States by Spain." Sumner did not examine the war in terms of whether the end justified the means. Nor did his case against U.S. military intervention overseas rest simply on the national interest. Instead, he appealed to America's revolutionary ideals, and he measured American actions against the nation's own patriotic standards. Said Sumner:

> My patriotism is of the kind which is outraged by the notion that the United States never was a great nation until in a petty three month's campaign it knocked to pieces a poor, decrepit, bankrupt old state like Spain. To hold such an opinion as that is to abandon all American standards, to put to shame and scorn all that our ancestors tried to build up here, and to go over to the standards of which Spain is a representative.

If one listens carefully, the arguments of the anti-imperialists of 1900 resonate in the criticisms of the Iraq war. However, so does the advocacy of those who favored national expansion, or what is now called pre-emptive action. In fact, American political leaders have acted "pre-emptively" since the earliest days of the Republic. Washington, D.C. has sent soldiers and marines against native insurgents in open rebellion on many occasions.

Western Hemisphere

The ideals that sent U.S. soldiers to the Philippines in 1898 also inspired American military interventions in the Western hemisphere. Indeed, John O'Sullivan's declaration of America's manifest destiny was meant originally for Mexico.

The 1848 Treaty of Guadalupe Hidalgo, which ended the Mexican war, confirmed Texas as a state and ceded California and

New Mexico to the U.S. Indeed, the aspiration to extend the American shade over Mexico never entirely disappeared. (The 1848 Democratic Party convention, flush with victory, demanded all of Mexico, and President Polk urged the occupation of Yucatan; ten years later President Buchanan similarly proposed that the U.S. occupy northern Mexico.) But sectional tensions prevented action and after the Civil War the U.S. was simply too exhausted to do more than urge France to abandon Maximilian to his fate in 1865.

Still, when American forces crushed the Spanish in Cuba in 1898 and intervened in Panama in 1903 it was clear that the U.S. viewed territory south of the border as its own special preserve. Between 1898 and 1933, the United States sent military forces into Latin American on at least twenty-five separate occasions. As in the Philippines, U.S. expeditionary forces were involved in military and paramilitary operations; they learned to fight guerrilla insurrectionists, improvising tactics against jungle and mountain irregulars.

American officials also learned how unpopular such conflicts were with the public, and how difficult it was to explain why military operations against guerrillas in such impoverished countries as Haiti and the Dominican Republic failed to produce results year after year.

During World War I, America's manifest destiny was put to the test—not in the trenches of France, but in the Caribbean. To halt civil wars and social anarchy America intervened in Haiti in 1915 and the Dominican Republic in 1916. Both conflicts resulted in long occupations—until 1924 in the Dominican Republic and 1934 in Haiti.

In 1926 the Coolidge Administration dispatched marines and bluejackets to Nicaragua to thwart an insurgency led by the guerrilla chieftain Augusto Sandino. It encountered an anti-war resistance not unlike the anti-imperialist movement of 1900. Nicaragua—like the Philippines earlier and Vietnam afterward— offers a historic example of the problems of strategy and politics inherent in any "imperial overstretch."

Between 1853 and 1925 the U.S. dispatched troops to Nicaragua on eleven occasions. In 1926 another of the country's chronic civil wars broke out and the U.S. went in a twelfth time.

Fearing an alleged Mexican plot to displace U.S. influence, President Coolidge told Congress, "I have the most conclusive evidence that arms and ammunition in large quantities have been, on several occasions since August 1926, shipped to the revolutionists in Nicaragua." This "evidence" never materialized and the Mexican "threat" disappeared. Coolidge and his successor Herbert Hoover found it harder than ever to explain their enterprise to an incredulous public and Congress.

The U.S., according to a *New York Times* correspondent, "ruled Nicaragua more completely than the American Federal Government rules any state in the Union." But the marines found it impossible to contain Sandino's guerrilla campaign. After seven frustrating years, the State Department sent out a memorandum stating that it preferred "to run the risk of revolutionary disturbances now and let the strong man emerge without further waste of time."

That's what happened. The U.S. hand-picked a *Guardia* chieftain, Anastasio Somoza, who, with his sons, dominated Nicaragua's politics until their dynasty was deposed by a second-generation of Sandinistas in 1979.

The Coolidge Administration recognized the futility of its own policies, and in 1928 it authorized a new policy directive ("the Clark Memorandum") restricting the application of the Monroe Doctrine to interference from Europe and not to disputes inside Latin America. After overseeing yet another Nicaraguan election, the Assistant Secretary of State for Latin America wrote, "I fervently hope that we will have no more elections in Latin America to supervise." After more than seven years of trying to restore order in that country, the military command was equally fatalistic. The marine commander wrote back to Washington that continuing occupation "would require many times the total available force of marines and *guardia,* and, in addition, would produce no definitive military results."

The Coolidge administration was backed into a tight political corner as prominent Republicans joined Democrats in Congress in opposing keeping U.S. forces in Nicaragua and the war against Sandino's guerillas. Challenging Administration arguments, Sen. William Borah (R-ID), chairman of the Senate Committee on Foreign Relations, proclaimed, "The truth is, effort is being made to get this country into a shameless, cowardly little war with

Mexico." Senator Burton K. Wheeler (D-MT) wondered if the Marines could "not be put to better use in Chicago?" Senator Clarence Dill (D-WA) labeled the intervention "one of the blackest and foulest crimes that has been committed against men." When members of both parties offered resolutions to withdraw U.S. troops and cut funding, Coolidge was forced to issue executive orders.

"Anti-imperialist" allegations of marine atrocities and Wall Street scandals occurred while fighting in Nicaragua continued. There were demonstrations in U.S. and foreign cities. Newspapers pressed the Administration for answers, and an editorial in the *Washington News* asked: "What is all this fighting about? Why are these young men in marine uniforms being killed?"

In these early military interventions, most American leaders failed to understand their enemy. Washington regarded peasant insurgents as bandits and urban rebels as criminals. But the Sandinistas had a worldwide political following and resisted the U.S. occupation for years. One dispatch by the U.S. Minister to Nicaragua is typical: "We may not see how the bandits can continue their depredations indefinitely in the face of such persecution as McDougal [Marine General Douglas McDougal] is giving them, but the fact remains that they do."

Only after the U.S. reevaluated its mission did authorities take into account Sandino's intentions. The U.S. *chargé* in Managua helped open Washington's eyes that the guerrilla war was "incidental to and derived from American assistance. In this connection it remains true that the avowed intention of Sandino ... is to eject the American forces from Nicaragua." The U.S. Minister later conceded "the possibility of conciliating Sandino will be greater if no marines remain in Nicaragua."

Political partisans defended and denounced the Administration's Nicaragua policy. One Marine Corps officer warned that public protest was "taken indeed as an indication of strong support for the forces arrayed against us, and thus serves to intensify and prolong the opposition we must overcome." But in 1929, one year after the issuance of the Clark Memorandum, the Assistant Secretary of State for Latin America announced that, "the sentiment in this country and especially in Congress is very strong against keeping the marines there indefinitely... we cannot indefinitely maintain a large force of marines in

Nicaragua." The same arguments were made over U.S. military presence in Vietnam—and in Iraq.

Henry L. Stimson, a towering Republican patriarch in his time, was twice Secretary of War (first under Taft and later for Franklin D. Roosevelt during World War II), and he served as Coolidge's private emissary to Nicaragua in 1927. At first, Stimson called for a U.S. military landing and he issued wildly over-confident cables predicting no opposition to a U.S. occupation. But by 1933, as Hoover's Secretary of State, Stimson was leading the call for withdrawal and was adamantly against further intervention in Latin America. Once asked if the U.S. would ever again send troops to Latin America, he replied:

Not on your life... It would undo all the labor of three years, and it would put me in absolute wrong in China, where Japan has done all of this monstrous work under the guise of protecting her nationals with a landing force.

U.S. intervention in Latin America in the early twentieth-century did not bring peace and security to the region despite America's best intentions. These episodes are largely forgotten today. But America's experience of fighting protracted and unpopular wars in backward areas for objectives that were nearly impossible to defend soon lost its luster. By the late 1920's the U.S. came to appreciate the need for positive and diplomatic solutions to the problems of the hemisphere. The incorporation of the "Good Neighbor" policy in Franklin Roosevelt's Inaugural Address led to an era of diplomatic initiatives undertaken in the 1930's that solidified the area against the original "Axis" of evil. The result was a hemisphere largely free from fascist intrusion during the World War II and, subsequently, the signing of the Rio Pact of 1947 and establishment of today's Organization of American States.

Chapter 4

FAILED PEACE STRATEGISTS: INTERNATIONALISTS AND NON-INTERVENTIONISTS

In 1910 the philosopher William James wrote "The Moral Equivalent of War," a seminal essay on the instinct for war. James argued that the prospect of war had a power to enchant men because it fulfilled certain basic aspirations such as their "contempt for softness, surrender of private interests and obedience to command." As a critic of America's intervention in Cuba and the Philippines, James searched for what he called a "moral equivalent" to war that would inspire manly pride, courage and loyalty to a higher cause than war. "So far," he wrote, "war has been the only force that can discipline a whole community and until an equivalent discipline is organized, I believe that war must have its way."

James had an alternative: It was to conscript American youth into a different kind of "army" that would fulfill a "disciplinary function." James' national service corps was akin to FDR's Civilian Conservation Corps or the Bush Administration's Americorps. He proposed to have young men harness their energies to control and improve nature, subduing the earth to the benefit of the community. The policy James advocated was a product of his philosophy of pragmatism. Reacting against messianic ideologies and belief systems that promised a way to attain universal ends, the pragmatist proposed methods to reach concrete and immediate results; he used ideas as "tools" and "instruments for coping."

James' colleague John Dewey compared ideas to hands. An idea, Dewey taught,

...has no greater metaphysical stature than, say, a fork. When your fork proves inadequate to the task of eating soup, it makes little sense to argue about whether there is something inherent in the nature of forks or something inherent in the nature of soup that accounts for the failure. You just reach for a spoon.

The American philosophy of pragmatism had considerable effect on advocates for peace. In his book *The Metaphysical Club* Louis Menand traces the impact of pragmatism on social ideas after the Civil War. He argues that James, Dewey, Oliver Wendell Holmes and other pragmatic-minded writers reacted against the anti-slavery crusades because they led to the Civil War, which had caused enormous human suffering. Because the abolitionists were dedicated to sweeping ideas of right and wrong they damaged the nation. Said Menand: They "had driven a wedge into white America, and they did it because they had become infatuated with an idea. They marched the nation to the brink of self-destruction in the name of an abstraction."

Pragmatic thinkers would not make that mistake. Using ideas as tools, they would enlist a new generation of men into a new army— one dedicated to peacemaking. Between the Civil War and World War I a new professional elite was in the making and it shaped new attitudes and policies toward war and peace. The new "establishment" elite was composed primarily of Republican officeholders, industrialists, Wall Street lawyers and conservative academics. These "wise men" would supervise American foreign policy over the course of most of the twentieth century—until the Vietnam War weakened their hold on power. Concentrated along the New York-to-Washington corridor, men like Elihu Root, Secretary of War (1899-1903) and State (1905-1909), and Henry Stimson, Secretary of War (1911-1913) and State (1929-1933), moved easily between private and government careers. They came to support American hegemony over the Philippines and Latin America, but they also believed in the importance of organizing treaties and institutions to guarantee international peace and order.

The new elite were pragmatists, not moralists. Concerned

mainly about the transatlantic world of U.S.-Europe relations, they tried to construct a world order in which peace and stability were necessary, whether moral or not. After all, the U.S. and Europe needed peace for trade and investment. Rid of the martial spirit of manifest destiny, U.S. foreign policymakers were a new breed of peace activist. They worked diligently to marshal public opinion to support diplomacy and international peacekeeping.

The new establishment supported America's entry into World War I in 1917. Like President Wilson, many endorsed the League of Nations. Philanthropist-industrialists such as John D. Rockefeller and Andrew Carnegie, college presidents like Stanford's David Starr Jordan and Columbia's Nicholas Murray Butler, and Republican establishment leaders such as John Hay and Charles Evans Hughes supported U.S. participation in a World Court and the codification of international law.

Even before Wilson proposed a League of Nations, the new leaders formed private groups to promote a new world order. In 1904 legislators around the world formed the Interparliamentary Union to spur the movement for peace. The Union promoted the Hague Tribunal to arbitrate disputes among nations and, with the endorsement of President Theodore Roosevelt, it called for a second Hague Conference to create an international court. In 1906 Nicholas Murray Butler organized the American Association for International Conciliation, and Andrew Carnegie became president of the New York Peace Society, second in size only to the American Peace Society.

In 1907, Carnegie and John D. Rockefeller underwrote a four-day National Arbitration and Peace Congress in New York, which was attended by over 40,000 people, making it the largest peace rally in U.S. history. Two years later, Carnegie allotted $10 million in U.S. Steel bonds to establish the Carnegie Endowment for International Peace. Elihu Root became its first president. From the beginning, the Endowment pursued a mission to "hasten the abolition of international war" through "scientific" studies of the causes and origins of war. It provided a non-governmental forum for men of affairs to meet and discuss world events (The terms "networking" and "NGO" were not yet in use). In Root's own expression, the Endowment was virtually a "division of the State Department, working in harmony constantly."

This type of practical organized peacekeeping dominated American foreign policy up to the brink of Pearl Harbor. Starting in 1908, policymakers searched for problem-solving mechanisms to ensure peace. They helped conclude World War I at Versailles, and they dominated the diplomacy of the 1920's and 1930's. In retrospect, it is no hyperbole to say that U.S. government policymakers during this period were the most powerful and productive force for opposing militarism and war and arguing for the peaceful settlement of disputes.

Of course, this approach to international policy failed. Indeed, observers hold it responsible for the failure of American preparedness that proved disastrous in December, 1941. George F. Kennan would later criticize the "legalistic-moralistic" approach to world politics:

> It is the belief that it should be possible to suppress the chaotic and dangerous aspirations of governments in the international field by the acceptance of some system of legal rules and restraints. This belief undoubtedly represents in part an attempt to transpose the Anglo-Saxon concept of individual law into the international field and to make it as applicable to governments as it is applicable here at home to individuals.

American policymakers were enthusiastic advocates of this approach. In 1908, Elihu Root engineered 24 bilateral arbitration treaties as President Roosevelt's Secretary of State. Three years later, President Taft concluded arbitration pacts with Britain and France that called for the submission of a full-range of issues to a Joint High Commission. (Taft later withdrew the agreements after the Senate insisted on attaching reservations to them.)

Liberal internationalism was at high tide when President Woodrow Wilson issued his Fourteen Points, which would conclude the Great War on terms that required old Europe to accept "open covenants of peace, openly arrived at." Enthusiasm ran high among many liberals who supported Wilson's war to end war. Assistant Secretary of War Raymond B. Fosdick directed a group of progressives that included James T. Shotwell of Columbia, Manley O. Hudson of Harvard, the journalist Walter Lippmann and Colonel Edward M. House, Wilson's closest aide.

Calling themselves "The Inquiry," the clandestine political cell met inside the White House to assist the President in devising a rational and scientific program to achieve global peace.

But Wilson failed to win Senate support for the League, and Warren Harding was elected president in 1920. This supposed "return to normalcy" is usually cited as evidence that U.S. foreign policy in the 1920's became "isolationist." This description is mistaken. In fact, Wilsonian legal internationalism reached new heights in theory and practice during the twenty years between the world wars.

The U.S. foreign policy of the era was intent on setting up an extraordinary arms control and peacekeeping regime "to make the world safe for democracy." By leading the peace movement, America's policymaking elite co-opted the ideals of dissident pacifists and socialists who were driven leftward into lonely opposition.

Disarmament

In the 1920's "peace" was a popular sentiment. It was an ideal promoted by mainstream Protestantism, which made room for liberal internationalism. There were regional and local "rallies for Peace," often held on church grounds. *The Christian Century,* a liberal journal, was widely-read, as were the works of the then-pacifist theologian Reinhold Niebuhr and YMCA leader and evangelist Sherwood Eddy. In 1923, Edward M. Bok, publisher of the *Ladies Home Journal,* offered a $100,000 "American Peace Award" for the best essay on America's role in international peace. The distinguished panel of judges included Henry L. Stimson, Colonel Edward House and Elihu Root. Eleanor Roosevelt was in charge of overseeing the 22,000 essays that swamped the Award's New York offices.

Interestingly, history's greatest advocate for world peace through negotiated arms reduction was not the Socialist party or a forerunner of Students for a Democratic Society. It was the Republican administration of Warren G. Harding. In December 1920, a month after Harding's election, Senator William Borah, an anti-League Idaho Republican, introduced a Senate resolution authorizing an international disarmament conference. The proposal was cheered by the public and press. In mid-1921, the conference received unanimous Senate endorsement and approval in the House with only four 'nays.' Harding's Secretary of State, Charles Evans Hughes, issued invitations and opened the nine-power conference in Washington on November 12, 1921. His address to the conference declared that the time for disarmament was "now."

Hughes proposed a ten-year "naval holiday" in the construction of capital ships (battleships and cruisers) and urged that ships in existence or under construction be scrapped so that the ship holdings of the U.S., Britain and Japan, the three great sea powers, could be capped to a ratio of 5-5-3. That meant the U.S. would have to destroy 30 of its capital ships, the British 19, and the Japanese 17. Hughes' speech "sunk" 66 capital ships—more, as one reporter wrote, "than all the admirals in the world have sunk in a cycle of centuries."

Widespread support in Congress for Hughes' proposals led to the Five Power Naval Treaty (including France and Italy), which was signed on February 6, 1922. It was supposed to remain in effect until 1936, when any power wishing to withdraw from the treaty was required to give a two-year notice. Other international agreements were subsequently negotiated, including a Four-Power Treaty on territorial stability in the Pacific (which replaced the Anglo-Japanese alliance of 1902) and a Nine-Power Treaty affirming the "Open Door" policy in China.

History records that the Washington Naval Disarmament Conference failed to achieve its goals. But at the time it was considered a landmark in world politics. Under the leadership of the United States, negotiation, arbitration and conciliation became the essential method for approaching issues of war and peace.

After Harding, U.S. foreign policy and diplomacy concentrated on disarmament. President Calvin Coolidge called for another naval conference in Geneva, Switzerland. His Secretary of State, Frank B. Kellogg, was not dismayed when negotiations broke down in August 1927 after six weeks of rancor. He simply initiated another round of arbitration treaties to replace those negotiated by Secretary Root in 1908-09. By

1931 the U.S. had signed 27 agreements with almost all the major powers.

By 1928 an international treaty to "outlaw" war found widespread U.S. public support. Petitions bearing two million signatures poured into Washington and forced the Coolidge Administration to float a proposal for such a document. Secretary Kellogg opened negotiations with the French foreign minister, Aristide Briand, for a bilateral pact to renounce war as "an instrument of national policy." The Pact of Paris, also known as the Kellogg-Briand Pact, was so popular it won Kellogg the 1929 Nobel Peace Prize.

The treaty—ultimately signed by 62 nations, including Germany and Japan—was the final monument to empty legalism and moralism in foreign policy. It permitted "defensive" war and authorized no sanctions against violations save the power of "world public opinion." But Coolidge advised Congress that the treaty would do "more for the peace of the world than any other agreement ever negotiated among the nations." The Senate ratified it 85 to 1.

Despite the Great Depression and the rise of fascism, the U.S. continued its quest for peace and disarmament through the holding of international conferences. President Herbert Hoover, another Republican, attended the 1930 Five-Power Naval Conference in London. It produced a limited treaty and led to still another conference in Geneva to discuss land-based disarmament.

The last of the great conferences was the General Disarmament Conference, which met from 1932 to 1937. It accomplished nothing and finished off the inter-war conferences for good. With Hitler in power, Germany demanded arms parity and France refused to consider disarmament without security guarantees. Japan had invaded Manchuria in 1931 and wanted to abrogate the Washington treaties altogether. According to historian Thomas A. Bailey, "Security-conscious nations felt that they would be wiser to sharpen their swords than to beat them into ploughshares."

The age of disarmament was ending, even for Americans. But Herbert Hoover took the moral high ground. Presiding over an Army that was smaller than Romania's (136,000 men) and a Navy that had scrapped fully 60 percent of its fleet, the Quaker president defended America's anti-war policies:

The colossal power of the United States overshadows scores of freedom-loving nations. Their defense against us is a moral defense. To give them confidence that with the higher moral sense of the American people this defense is more powerful than all armies or navies, is a sacred duty which lies upon us.

Isolationism

The world was in crisis and disarmament was discredited. What would the United States do? Taking the initiative, members of the U.S. Congress concluded that if there was to be a foreign war, Americans should stay out of it.

In 1934, a North Dakota Republican, Senator Gerald Nye, opened an investigation into whether bankers and munitions manufacturers were responsible for U.S. involvement in World War I. The "Nye hearings" created a national sensation. Committee investigators uncovered evidence of collusion between U.S. and British firms prior to the U.S. declaration of war. They also alleged excessive business lobbying for higher arms budgets, extraordinary arms profits and corruption. The publication that year of *Merchants of Death,* a study of the international arms industry by journalist Frank Hanighen, further heightened hostility to business. It was followed by Marine General Smedley Butler's 1935 article "War is a Racket," which was condensed by *Reader's Digest* and widely distributed.

War is a racket. It always has been. It is possibly the oldest, easily the most profitable, surely the most vicious. It is the only one international in scope. It is the only one in which the profits are reckoned in dollars and the losses in lives.... It is conducted for the benefit of the very few, at the expense of the very many. Out of war a few people make huge fortunes.

The historian Charles A. Beard published *The Devil Theory of War* (1936). It was a variation on the Nye Committee report, arguing that U.S. economic policies pushed the Wilson Administration into war. Beard claimed to show a link between

American prosperity and allied war orders: "If the war stopped," he wrote, "American business would slow down from prosperity to dullness, if not calamity. If the Allies were defeated, things would be worse. American millions were at stake."

The drumbeat of opposition to war led Congress to pass the Neutrality Act in August 1935. It required the President to impose an impartial embargo on all belligerent states in case of war. It also authorized the President to warn Americans against travel on belligerent ships and established a National Munitions Control Board to license and supervise arms exports. A series of amended neutrality acts followed. Then in 1937 Rep. Louis Ludlow, an Indiana Democrat, introduced a constitutional amendment requiring a national referendum for war (absent a foreign invasion). The amendment was narrowly defeated in the House, 209-188, after a lobbying blitz against it by President Roosevelt and despite the strong support of pacifist, neutralist and isolationist groups. Only three years before Pearl Harbor, a switch of eleven votes would have stripped the President and Congress of their constitutional war-making duties.

In 1940-1941, with Europe at war, the Roosevelt Administration attempted to help Great Britain, providing it with military goods and services under the Lend-Lease Act. But large numbers of Americans denounced what they considered a rush to war. Some were anti-British and anti-FDR, others pro-German and anti-Semitic. Father Charles Coughlin, the Catholic "radio priest," held over 30 million listeners spellbound with his anti-war tirades. ("Must the entire world go to war for 600,000 Jews in Germany?")

However, many Americans were simply anxious to stay out of another war. The most prominent of the isolationist groups was America First, which was formed in 1940 by the liberal journalist John T. Flynn, the progressive Philip La Follette, a former Wisconsin governor and son of the famous "Fighting Bob," and General Robert E. Wood, a former president of Sears, Roebuck. Its great spokesman was Charles A. Lindbergh, the "Lone Eagle" aviator. John F. Kennedy and Gerald R. Ford were youthful members.

For a time the American Communist Party (CPUSA) appeared to make an unholy alliance with Father Coughlin and America First. Between August 1939 and June 1941, Hitler and

Stalin were allies, dividing Poland between them and allowing Nazi Germany to focus its attack on France and Britain. During this period the Communist party and its fellow travelers were devoted to "peace." Claiming that Britain was waging an "imperialist war," the CPUSA went to great lengths to hamper Roosevelt's pro-British initiatives. Communist "front groups" demonstrated against war while pro-Communist union leaders tried to shut down defense plants, requiring Washington to dispatch troops to re-open them.

However, when Germany invaded the Soviet Union on June 22, 1941 the Communist party-line made a U-turn overnight. One Communist front, *The American Peace Mobilization,* changed its name to *The American People's Mobilization for Victory Over Nazism.* After Pearl Harbor, the CPUSA became entirely patriotic. (As we have seen, the flexibility of Communist tactics dominates the modern "peace" movement.) As for America First: it honorably disbanded on December 11, 1941, issuing a statement that "the time for military action is here."

Pearl Harbor fractured the peace movement. The hard-core pacifist groups, such as the Fellowship of Reconciliation (FOR), Women's International League for Peace and Freedom (WILPF), and the War Resisters League (WRL) remained adamant against the struggle. But most Americans, left and right, supported the war effort without major reservations.

Peace Activism After 1945

World War II demonstrated the failure of both the internationalists' dream of a system of negotiated treaties and the isolationists' stubborn unwillingness to confront an aggressor. Neither could prevent war. Despite defeating Germany and Japan, the United States now faced an aggressive Soviet Union. Americans were forced to return to the issue of war and peace. What conditions led to war? What could produce a lasting peace?

Some analysts think the problem is the nation-state. It has endured—indeed, flourished—over three centuries of continuous warfare. But for peace to prevail, they argue that there needs to be world government in some form. Strobe Talbott, a former undersecretary of state in the Clinton Administration and currently president of the Brookings Institution, has said, "I'll bet that within the next hundred years,… nationhood as we know it will be obsolete; all states will recognize a single authority… All countries are basically social arrangements, accommodations to changing circumstances. No matter how permanent and even sacred they may seem at any one time, in fact they are all artificial and temporary."

Talbott's prediction reflects the dream of liberal internationalists who fear political anarchy above all else. Albert Einstein's foreboding words still haunt most liberals: "In relations among nations complete anarchy still prevails. I do not believe that we have made any real progress in this area during the last few thousand years."

After 1945 peace activists tried to overcome the problem of the nation-state by proposing alternative institutions to satisfy the need for world government. The United Nations was an answer for some, but it did not satisfy all internationalists, who remembered the doomed League of Nations. They wanted something more.

The most sophisticated indictment of the nation-state system was *The Anatomy of Peace* (1945) by a now-forgotten writer named Emery Reves. It was the intellectual guide for what became known as the world federalist movement. "Let us be clear about one thing," Reves wrote," a league of sovereign nation-states is not a step… toward peace. Peace is law. The San Francisco league [the UN] is the pitiful miscarriage of the Second World War… Equal and sovereign power units can never, under any circumstances, under any conditions, coexist peacefully." The *The Anatomy of Peace* was translated into 25 languages and lauded by Einstein, who called it "the political answer to the atomic bomb."

World government advocates claimed the moral high ground after Hiroshima and Nagasaki. Robert M. Hutchins, president of the University of Chicago, would write, "The survival of mankind demands a world community, a world government and a world state." Retired Supreme Court justice Owen Roberts called for "a parliament of the world" else we face "the constant peril of utter destruction." Historian Carl Van Doren wrote, "We cannot afford the luxury of national rivalry and jealousy running wild in a world that holds the atom bomb."

In October 1945, fifty prominent Americans met at Dublin, New Hampshire for a conference on world government hosted by Justice Roberts. Their final report criticized the inadequacy of the U.N. and endorsed "a world federal government...with closely defined and limited power adequate to prevent war." (The signers included Lt. Kingman Brewster, Jr., a future Yale president, and Sgt. Alan Cranston, a future California Senator.) Fourteen state legislatures passed resolutions for world government by 1946; the authors of one study described the proliferation of world government groups as "so great as to defy even listing." A 1946 poll found that 54 percent of Americans favored a global authority of some kind to control the world's armies. "The feeling that the United Nations is hopelessly weak," wrote New York University professor Clyde Eagleton, "is widespread in the United States."

The Women's International League for Peace and Freedom (WILPF), Norman Thomas' Socialist Party and the Federal Council of Churches urged the U.S. Senate to ratify the UN charter. But many peace activists were in an awkward position. The Rev. Harry Emerson Fosdick, a noted pacifist and minister at New York City's Riverside Church, warned, "We who wanted a better outcome will turn perfectionist and... will join up with the isolationists... and that between us no world organization will be accepted by the Senate."

In April 1947 world government groups met in Asheville, North Carolina, to form the United World Federalists (UWF). UWF aimed to mobilize grassroots support and lobby for "world peace through world law." In 1949, it claimed 720 local chapters in 31 states, with a national membership of 45,000. But the cause of "world federalism" inspired no populist movement. It tended to attract high-minded Establishment figures of the era like Connecticut Governor Chester Bowles, *Saturday Review* editor Norman Cousins, and General Electric chairman Owen D. Young.

The most forceful advocates of world government and atomic disarmament were the scientists who felt most responsible for the atomic age. Convinced that they were "naturally appointed guardians" of peace in a new era, Manhattan Project scientists formed the Federation of Atomic Scientists (FAS) in 1945 and published *the Bulletin of the Atomic Scientists.* By 1948 FAS was organized into four local associations and claimed 3000 members. They sought civilian control over the U.S. atomic energy program and an international program to control its development.

However, after the Soviet Union vetoed a U.S. plan to internationalize the development and use of atomic energy (the Baruch Plan), the scientists' effort quickly lost public support and political credibility. By 1948-49, with the fall of Czechoslovakia to communism, the Berlin airlift, and the formation of NATO, the peace movement was on the defensive. For the next fifteen years, liberal internationalists and atomic scientists were unable to organize a substantial peace movement. The Cold War had institutionalized alliance blocs and given credibility to theories of balance-of-terror and nuclear deterrence.

Opponents of Cold War, Left and Right

American peace politics was frustrated. For a time isolationists and leftist progressives tried offering alternatives to the emerging bipartisan consensus on foreign policy. They made strange bedfellows—conservatives such as *Chicago Tribune* publisher Robert McCormick and Illinois Republican representative Everett M. Dirksen and progressives like New York City mayor Fiorello La Guardia and Senators Claude Pepper (D-FL) and Glen Taylor (D-ID) warned against the new foreign policy consensus. They feared it would undermine American democracy, bankrupt the economy, upset the Constitution's checks and balances, and lead to "militarism."

The so-called "isolationists" on the right took their bearings from Washington's Farewell Address and the security of American geography. The America First Committee was their vehicle before World War II. Historian Ronald Radosh notes:

These conservatives raised issues and defined problems that... opened the way for liberals and leftist critics of a future epoch. They offered theories to account for American expansionism; they warned against the erosion of congressional powers by the executive; they opposed military intervention abroad, and criticized what they candidly termed the emergence of American imperialism.

105

Pearl Harbor effectively silenced America First, but after the war Senator Robert Taft (R-OH) and his colleagues on the Republican right resurrected the idea of "nonintervention." On the issue of U.S. overseas intervention, Taft—known as "Mr. Republican"—departed from the Truman Administration and the mainly eastern Republicans who supported the President. A powerful figure of dissent, he has been described as either a traditional isolationist or as a "conservative nationalist," fiercely anti-communist but libertarian, and opposed to what President Eisenhower later termed the "military-industrial complex."

"Taft Republicans" opposed Lend-Lease before the U.S. entered World War II. After the war, they opposed NATO and the claim that the president had the authority to station troops in Europe. Later Taft opposed the Korean War, deepening U.S. engagements in Asia, and a Cold War rhetoric that cast the U.S. as the "world's policeman." Taft's foreign policy outlook was decidedly out of step with post-war liberalism. Shortly before his death in 1953 he had to admit that he had been "pretty well over-ruled by opinion among both Democrats and Republicans."

Taft deplored *Time* magazine publisher Henry Luce's call for an "American Century." He deplored attempts to impose on "foreign peoples through the use of American money, and even perhaps American arms, the policies which moral leadership is able to advance only through the sound strength of its principles." He saw no purpose for America to engage distant regions in the Far East: "I certainly do not think," he said at the height of the Korean War, "that we should be obligated to send American troops to defend Indo-china or Burma or Thailand where they would become involved in a much more serious war than we have been forced into in Korea."

In April 1949 Taft was one of fourteen Senators voting against ratification of the North Atlantic Treaty. "The Atlantic Pact," he judged, "...obligates us to go to war if at any time during the next twenty years anyone makes an armed attack on any of the twelve nations." He found NATO "unnecessarily extensive." "I am opposed," he stated in a major address, to the whole idea of giving the President power to arm the world against Russia or anyone else, or even to arm Western Europe, except where there is a real threat of aggression. We are stimulating an armament race. We are trying to restore a military balance of power on the European continent. Such policies in the past have always led to war rather than peace."

On Truman's left, there also was opposition. Henry Wallace, Roosevelt's Vice-President and later Secretary of Commerce, led those who saw little threat from Communism and protested U.S. responses to actions by the Soviet Union. Said Wallace in a famous September 12, 1946 speech in Madison Square Garden: "The Russians should stop conniving against us in certain areas just as we should stop scheming against them in other parts of the world." Wallace added that the U.S "should recognize that we have no more business in the political affairs of Eastern Europe than Russia has in the political affairs of Latin America." A few days later Wallace was ousted from Truman's cabinet, setting the stage for his failed 1948 presidential campaign.

Wallace also opposed NATO. He thought the alliance would "lead only to national insolvency, the surrender of our traditional freedoms, war, a possible military disaster, and the certain sacrifice not only of life and treasure but of the very system of government which it is supposed to preserve."

But Taft and Wallace were no match for Truman. More importantly, neither was willing to oppose his government in wartime. Taft faulted Truman's policies in Korea, but supported General Douglas MacArthur's offensive and urged "every possible means to drive the Chinese Communists from Korea." Wallace, too, supported the war effort, announcing in 1950, "When my country is at war... I am on the side of my country... I cannot agree with those who want to start a propaganda drive to pull the UN troops out of Korea."

Still, the emerging Cold War policies of military aid and foreign intervention troubled many Americans. Legislators often did not want to admit the long-term consequences of their new policies. They resorted to anti-war rhetoric to disguise or deny them.

A case-in-point: the Senate debate over the North Atlantic Treaty. Despite the reality of Cold War conflict, the Truman administration endorsed NATO as a force for collective peace, referring to it grandly in Wilsonian terms. The State Department even prepared Administration witnesses with materials describing NATO as an instrument for a "balance of principle."

NATO was said to be "an alliance against war itself." Warren

Austin, Truman's Ambassador to the United Nations (and a former Republican Senator from Vermont), told the Senate Foreign Relations Committee that NATO was *not* a military alliance. Instead, it was meant "to maintain international peace and security." Appealing to an historic American revulsion against power politics, Austin said NATO opened a new era of "power for peace. And out went old man balance of power." This played well on Capitol Hill:

> THE CHAIRMAN [Sen. Tom Connally (D-TX)]: *As a matter of fact, this treaty is not a general military alliance in any sense. It is limited to defense against armed attack.*
> THE SECRETARY [of Defense, Louis Johnson]: *That is right, sir.*
> THE CHAIRMAN: *it is the very opposite of the military alliance.*
> SENATOR TYDINGS: *Defensive entirely.*
> THE CHAIRMAN: *Defensive entirely. It is an alliance of peace, if you want to call it an alliance.*
> THE SECRETARY: *I like your language.*
> THE CHAIRMAN: *It is an alliance against armed attack, it is an alliance against war, and does not partake of the essentials of the primary obligation of a military alliance as we know military alliances at all; is that true?*
> THE SECRETARY: *That is right, sir.*

NATO passed the Senate and "containment," the term coined by George F. Kennan in 1947, became the guidepost shaping America's foreign policies for the next thirty-five years. Yet a new and highly-charged "conservative movement" also began to take shape at this time. Opposed to both Taft's isolationism and Truman's containment, it was born out of frustration over the "loss" of China to communism in 1949 and by revelations that Soviet spies had transferred U.S. atomic secrets to Moscow.

At the 1952 Republican convention, this party faction called for a "rollback" of Soviet power in eastern Europe and a global American offensive against world communism. Communism was singular and aggressive, it warned, and containment was defensive and would lead to an American defeat. Championed by William F. Buckley, Jr. and his "New Right" journal, *National Review*, the movement reached a peak during the 1964 presidential campaign of Arizona Senator Barry Goldwater. As argued in his book, *The Conscience of a Conservative* (New York: Victor, 1960), the strategy of containment was unable to address a communist offensive:

> Now, while traitors... have at times occupied key positions in our government, it is clear that our national leadership over the past fourteen years has favored neither surrender nor treason. It is equally clear, however, that our leaders have not made victory the goal of American policy. And the reason that they have not done so, I am saying, is that they have never believed deeply that the Communists are in earnest.

Goldwater was crushed by the incumbent president, Lyndon Johnson, but electoral defeat merely forced the conservative movement to focus more clearly on a political strategy of grassroots organizing. It eventually paid off in the presidential election of Ronald Reagan in 1980. Reagan's policies toward the Soviet Union were the direct byproduct of Goldwater's dissent from 1960's containment policies and led to the implosion of Soviet power in 1991. "Mr. Gorbachev, tear down this wall," Reagan's inspiring demand, was a product of what can fairly be termed the most successful grassroots political protest in American history.

Visions of Western Unity

The conservative movement taking shape in the 1960's was not narrowly nationalistic. Books like James Burnham's *Suicide of the West* (New York: John Day, 1964) opposed containment and urged a revival of Western Civilization. Liberals also wanted to create global movements rising above the confines of the nation-state. The idea that a world community could create world peace if only national leaders would submit their policies to some sort of "global test" intoxicated many.

That was the attitude underpinning the United Nations conferences that played such a large role in the 1990s. At these conferences, so-called "civil society" movements were organized worldwide around such issues as the environment, gender equity, population control, and, perhaps most importantly, arms control. They argued that modern technology and political change were so complex that isolated nation-states could no longer meet their people's needs. The parochial talents of politicians and diplomats were inadequate to human needs. Public problems required cooperative action across national boundaries handled by highly trained specialists with technical skills.

This vision of a coordinated global society is discernible in a 1943 book entitled *A Working Peace System* by David Mitrany (1888-1975), a Romanian scholar living in England. Mitrany attempted to outline the idea that all human and material resources could be progressively integrated. By harmonizing mankind's social and economic "functions," Mitrany believed peace and progress would replace war.

It was clear to Mitrany in 1943 that nationalism and national interest, patriotism and ideology were all manifestations of the old order. They had to be replaced by a "world community" held together by a web of institutions. Mitrany conceived that a process he called ramification would develop a concentric-circle growth of institutions. Over time they would change attitudes and replace old loyalties. The first step was gradually to replace nation-based armaments with a system of global arms controllers who represented multilateral interests. Mitrany came to see European integration, beginning with the creation of the Coal and Steel Community in 1951 and leading to the Common Market in the 1960's (and eventually the European Union) as marks of "a working peace system."

The unity of the western democracies is an idea with a long history. The nineteenth century French historian Jules Michelet, fearing Russia, appealed to America and Europe for unity:

I call here to a European Congress ... the English, the French, the Belgians, the Dutch, the Swiss, I call the Germans. I call here the two worlds. I solemnly call upon young America. Let her justify our hope, let her be deaf to all the petty interests, free of all petty rancours, devoted to the great general interest of all human progress, closely associated with the civilized west, with the same cause of liberty which she has supported so recently and which she has made so gloriously victorious.

In 1910, Norman Angell wrote *The End of Illusion,* an attempt

110

to demonstrate that Europe's economic integration would make future wars impossible. And in 1938 American journalist Clarence K. Streit wrote *Union Now*, drawing on American federalism to make the case for an Atlantic federation: "Can we hope to find a safer, surer, more successful way than this? What democrat among us does not hope that this union will be made some day? What practical man believes it will ever be made by mere dreaming or that the longer we delay starting to make it the sooner we shall have it? "

World War II did not destroy Streit's faith in an idea that, some sixty years later, seems hopelessly utopian. Yet practical men and women have embraced it. Walter Lippmann, who advised Wilson at Versailles, wrote during World War II that the democracies "should consolidate the strategic and diplomatic connections already existing, of the Atlantic Community." Today, its closest approximation is NATO, a military alliance formed in 1949 and still evolving as an association of sovereignties, which includes those whose eastern borders touch on Russia.

A union of the democracies as an answer to the quest for "world order" can still inspire. The late Robert Strausz-Hupé (1903-2002), who left his native Austria after the Nazi takeover in 1938 to teach at the University of Pennsylvania and eventually become a U.S. ambassador to five posts, including NATO and Turkey, never lost sight of the ideal. The author of seminal works on international relations, geopolitics and political philosophy, this conservative academic supported Barry Goldwater in 1964 and Ronald Reagan in 1980. In 1995, he wrote his last book in tribute to Alexis de Tocqueville. "The time has come," Strausz-Hupé concluded,

for leveling with the country and the world, and to state, in language understandable to all, the purpose of American foreign policy. Now less than ever can American democracy tolerate a world half free and half unfree. To abdicate from its mission as the federating power of democracy would be not only a colossal strategic blunder but also a betrayal of the ideals that led American democracy from a remote corner of the globe to the heights of world power.

Can this ideal survive in our age of ideologies, which begins with Marxism-Leninism and now flourishes in the fanaticism of radical Islam? America's peace movement took a sharp left turn when our country entered the mainstream of power politics during the Cold War. But clearly, neither the liberal internationalist vision of a new world order nor the underground left-wing revolution conspiring against it holds out much promise.

Chapter 5

THE ORIGINS OF THE ANTI-WAR LEFT

Both liberal internationalists and conservative non-interventionists failed to produce effective peace policies. However sincere their motives and well-developed their ideas, these peace strategists did not create peace in the twentieth century, the world's bloodiest. That created an opening for the Left, a political force that wreaked havoc on the twentieth century.

The Left in America comprises a tiny sliver of public life, but it is unmatched in its zeal for radical causes and for its devotion to political organizing and activism. The current "anti-war" movement is a creation of the Left, which is dedicated to social upheaval and revolutionary politics. How did such a movement manage to portray itself as dedicated to peace?

The Radical Left

World War I launched the modern American Left. Splinter groups of feminists, socialists and pacifists refused to support U.S. entry into the war or President Woodrow Wilson's plans for a post-war League of Nations. Their leaders did not trust Wilson's promises of a lasting peace. Unlike the conservative nationalists in the Senate, who thought the League went too far in compromising American sovereignty, the anti-war activists of the Left refused to support the League because it didn't go far enough. Their peace agenda called for an end to "militarism," "capitalism," "imperialism" and "nationalism."

The Wilson Administration and its Republican successors reacted fiercely to the new groups, which were inspired by the Bolshevik Revolution. During the war and in the 1920's leftist groups were marginalized and repressed by Attorney General A. Mitchell Palmer and J. Edgar Hoover, head of the Justice Department's General Intelligence Division and subsequently legendary head of the FBI. In 1917 the administration passed the Espionage Act, which provided stiff punishments for "false statements" and the "attempt to cause insubordination, disloyalty, mutiny or refusal of duty." Not a single German spy was convicted by the act, but hundreds of anti-war dissenters were seized, jailed or deported. On September 3, 1917 the headquarters of the Industrial Workers of the World (IWW) were raided in 33 U.S. cities, and over 100 leaders were arrested. The socialist leader, Eugene V. Debs, drew a ten-year jail sentence for an anti-war speech in Canton, Ohio in 1918. In 1919-1920 Attorney General Palmer supervised the round-up of over 6,000 suspected radicals. In December 1919, 249 aliens were deported on the ship *Buford* to the Soviet Union. They included anarchist Emma Goldman, who had set up "No Conscription" leagues. The following year a bomb blast on Wall Street killed 38 people and injured hundreds more. New York City had its first brush with modern terrorism.

Few Americans paid attention to Leftist ideologues in the 1920's. But in the 1930's the Left found an audience with the onset of the Great Depression. Like the current generation of protest leaders, the "Old Left" of the 1930's looked to Karl Marx and the promise of Communism to explain and transform world events. Leftist activists denied the values of American society and challenged the premises of American history.

However, the Left's view of war and peace during the 1930's oscillated with the tide of politics. The "party line" changed with every change in Soviet foreign policy. Leftists typically believed Western capitalism produced war. But when Hitler rose to power the Left quickly lost interest in peace advocacy. Communists joined socialists and liberals in a "Popular Front" that extolled American democracy; they called for military aid to resist Hitler and wanted to help the Spanish Republic in its civil war against Franco.

But when the Soviet Union announced that it had signed a non-aggression pact with Hitler in August 1939, the Communist

Party of the United States (CPUSA) did an about-face. Once again it became an advocate for peace and a stern critic of the Western "capitalist" powers. That changed yet again in June 1941 when Hitler betrayed his ally and invaded the Soviet Union. Suddenly the CPUSA turned pro-war and became a defender of the Western "democracies."

Conscientious Objectors in World War II

After Pearl Harbor almost all Americans favored war. Probably never before or since has the nation been so united. There was no anti-war movement during World War II. The only hold-outs were the conscientious objectors. Opposed to fighting World War II, "CO's" would become veterans—of the Civilian Public Service Camps (CPS) and the federal prison system.

During World War II there were 37,000 opponents of conscription and war who performed some type of alternative service. Most of these "conscientious objectors," or "COs," were assigned to 151 CPS camps built by the government. The system worked well enough. The federal government wanted to keep COs out of sight so as not to lower public morale, while the traditional peace churches—the Quakers, Mennonites, and Church of the Brethren—wanted to protect COs from public attacks.

However, by the end of the war many COs were rebelling against the CPS system. Not only were they paid no wages, but many objected that the Selective Service would not credit their idealism. Their complaint was summarized in an open letter: "We consider conscription to be a process of involuntary servitude," it said, "which denies the freedom for occupational choice basic to democracy." In a congressional hearing, U.S. Senator Mon Wallgren (D-WA) told the Selective Service chief, General Lewis B. Hershey, "You are treating these fellows worse than Japs."

Embittered, U.S. conscientious objectors began to initiate camp walkouts and labor strikes. A tiny core, alienated from traditional religious anti-war groups and pacifist societies, was attracted to the tactics of non-cooperative resistance inspired by India's Mahatma Gandhi. Said one, "Western pacifism has too long depended on individual conscience. We must now develop group non-violent action to effectively build a peaceful society."

A smaller group of 6,000 conscientious objectors were sent to federal prison. During World War II, every sixth man in federal prison was a conscientious objector. Many led uprisings there, such as one at the Danbury, Connecticut federal prison in April 1943. CO work strikes and hunger strikes plagued other prisons, including those in Lewisburg, Pennsylvania, Ashland, Kentucky and Petersburg, Virginia, creating situations, said one authority, which "approached full rebellion."

As pacifists began to see themselves as political rebels, they created new organizations and publications. One called for the formation of "a revolutionary pacifist group which renounces the class and caste structure of our society just as clearly as it renounces war." The pacifist draft resister George Houser proposed a new group named "Non-Violent Direct Actionists." He had joined the Fellowship of Reconciliation and War Resisters League, and spent a year in Danbury prison for draft resistance. Writer Dwight MacDonald endorsed radical pacifism as a way to attain revolutionary goals. He quit the radical and pro-war *Partisan Review* in 1943 and founded a little magazine named *Politics* (1943-1949), which attracted left-wing intellectuals such as the sociologist C. Wright Mills and writers David Bazelon and Paul Goodman.

Radical pacifists organized tax-avoidance protests and demonstrated against military conscription. They would serve as models for some war resisters in the 1960's. A few even became a part of the New Left anti-war movement. David Dellinger, a World War II conscientious objector, was the oldest member of the "Chicago Seven," the anti-war agitators (who included Tom Hayden, Abbie Hoffman and Jerry Rubin) who were tried for inciting riots at the 1968 Democratic National Convention in Chicago.

Towards a New Left

Conscientious objectors were a tiny minority during World War II. In the 1950s they, along with other peace activists and radical pacifists, were unable to sustain an anti-war movement. The Cold War created a bipartisan consensus on foreign policy that destroyed any peace movements such as those that flourished in the 1920's and 1930's. Leftist activists redirected their attention to such issues as domestic security. They denounced the McCarren Act (which made Communist party membership a crime) and the Smith Act (which outlawed advocating the overthrow of the U.S. government). They also called for abolition of the House Committee on Un-American Activities (HUAC) and circulated amnesty petitions for jailed and indicted Communist Party members. In general, peace activists became less concerned with war and more concerned about "McCarthyism."

By the mid-1950's the public generally associated peace movement groups with the Communist Party. HUAC called the Fellowship of Reconciliation, which was founded in 1915, an authentic pacifist group, but warned that it believed "class war was necessary." The American Council of Christian Laymen bluntly labeled it a "radical-pacifist group using Christian terms to spread Communist propaganda." The War Resisters League (founded in 1923) was cited as a co-sponsor of "Communist-controlled movements."

Some religion-based peace societies refused to back down and continued to promote non-violent action as a tactic. "The way to vote for peace," one Peacemakers pamphlet instructed, "was to act and live peace....[refuse] to be drafted for suicidal atomic and biological war, to make war weapons or to pay taxes for these weapons." But political events were changing these groups. In *Peace and Revolution: The Moral Crisis of American Pacifism* (1988), historian Guenther Lewy dissected the political descent of four once-eminent pacifist groups: the American Friends Service Committee, the War Resisters League, the Fellowship of Reconciliation, and the Women's International League for Peace and Freedom. The impact of the Vietnam War, he wrote, contributed to their leftward shift more than any other event. Once committed to religious pacifism the groups drifted toward support for Communist-led revolution. Lewy lamented the transition:

Over the past twenty years American pacifism has undergone a remarkable transformation. While at one time pacifists were single-mindedly devoted to the principles of nonviolence and reconciliation,

117

today most pacifist groups defend the moral legitimacy of armed struggle and guerrilla warfare, and they praise and support the communist regimes emerging from such conflicts.

Authors G. Russell Evans and C. Gregg Singer also charted the deterioration of pacifist belief. Their 1983 book *The Church and the Sword* surveyed what twenty-three mainline Protestant churches in the National and World Council of Churches had to say about pacifism. It found that many church leaders equated theological opposition to war with a secular and humanist accommodation to Communism. "This study is intended to present, as factually and accurately as possible," they began,

...the involvement of the mainline churches and their councils and leaders in unilateral disarmament, pacifist movements, and other anti-defense activities. The aggregate result of these programs has been to weaken the security of the United States in a time of great national peril; or more accurately, these activities have helped create the national peril. Moreover, many coincided with the objectives of the communists in their quest for world domination, and a shocking number of their ideas have been adopted by the various federal administrations.

David Dellinger founded the magazine *Liberation* in 1956. Like MacDonald's *Politics* it became a publishing outlet for a cadre of committed left-wing peace radicals. The articles it published represented a coming-of-age for the World War II era pacifists who had been COs. Peace activists now focused on themes that have since come to dominate the Left: anti-capitalism, anti-militarism, civil rights, and third world liberation.

Anti-nuclear activism was added to the mix with the formation in 1957 of SANE (Committee for a Sane Nuclear Policy). SANE joined radicalized social activists to members of the United World Federalists, who cultivated a "responsible" image. Homer Jack, SANE's executive director, referred to SANE as "pragmatic, not absolutist."

The issue of nuclear disarmament drew peace activists to SANE and to other groups on the left like the Committee for Non-Violent Action (CNVA), whose members engaged in illegal disruption, including entering nuclear weapons test ranges. Their arrests brought more publicity to the movement and attracted a new generation to the anti-war cause.

An act of defiance by A. J. Muste, an iconic figure of the old peace movement, marked the transition from the old to the new activism. In 1959 townspeople looked on as TV cameras filmed the 75-year-old Muste and two others climb over a fence at the Mead ICBM base west of Omaha, Nebraska. They were promptly arrested. "Omaha Action" was sponsored by CNVA; for days afterwards groups of pacifists illegally entered the missile base and were thrown in jail. All, including Muste, received suspended sentences. However, Omaha Action was a dividing line between the old and new forms of protest. To paraphrase President Kennedy's inaugural address, the "torch had been passed to a new generation" of anti-war protesters.

A.J. Muste and SANE's politics of nuclear disarmament represented the failed activism of the early Cold War years. Connecticut Democratic Senator Thomas Dodd would charge SANE with falling under Communist influence. But by 1959-1960 a new gathering of activists—students, intellectuals and feminists—was organizing along new lines. They would lead the demonstrations of the middle and late 1960's.

Students for a Democratic Society

The early 1960s saw the formation of the Student Peace Union (SPU), the era's first major student anti-war organization. In Washington, the socialist feminist Dagmar Wilson formed Women Strike for Peace. In 1961, 77-year-old Norman Thomas started Turn Toward Peace, a coalition of nearly forty peace, church and labor organizations. During World War I Thomas was the spokesman for the Fellowship of Reconciliation. He became nationally famous, lecturing from coast to coast: "You cannot conquer war by war; cast out Satan by Satan; or do the enormous evil of war that good may come." Thomas was the Socialist Party's candidate for president six times from 1924 to 1948.

However, the turning point for anti-war politics was the creation of Students for a Democratic Society, also known as SDS. An outgrowth of the League for Industrial Democracy, a tiny socialist group whose roots went back to the early years of the century, SDS became the unifying force of the New Left in the early and mid-1960's. SDS members were initially active in the civil rights movement. But under the leadership of Tom Hayden, SDS focused on issues of war and peace.

In 1962 Hayden drafted the *Port Huron Statement,* probably the most significant document of the New Left movement. It offered college-age young people a radical vision that linked a humanistic philosophy to a sweeping condemnation of American foreign and military policies: "We would replace power rooted in possession, privilege or circumstances by power and uniqueness rooted in love, reflectiveness, reason and creativity... As a social system we seek the establishment of a democracy of individual participation." The slogans of a generation—"Make Love, Not War" and "participatory democracy" were products of the New Left "counter-culture."

Scholars have described the 1960's counter-culture as a product of generational change. Michael Walzer put the Sixties into historical perspective, comparing the moment to the Puritan, French and Russian revolutions.

All forms of radical politics make their appearance at moments of rapid and decisive change, moments when customary status is in doubt and character (or "identity") is itself a problem... There is a point in the modernization process when large numbers of men, suddenly masterless, seek a rigid self-control; when they discover new purposes, dream of a new order, organize their lives for disciplined and methodical activity. These men are prospective saints and citizens.

Political scientist Suzanne Berger argued that generational protest in the 1960's was a reaction to the demand for success that postindustrial America made upon its young. The young, she explained, were not merely protesting the war or the government or social inequality. The peace movement was "not against the failure of the state and society to provide for economic growth and material prosperity, but against their all-too considerable success in having done so, and against the price of this success." Burdened by wealth and prosperity, the young joined the peace movement to attack the state as an "imperial" behemoth that smothered societies at home and abroad and was intolerant of deviation.

120

UC Berkeley philosopher Lewis Feuer saw the darker essence of that cause. To challenge this state of affairs, the young created a political movement that was becoming, in Leninist terms, a "cell" lacking in toleration. It was becoming like past revolutionary movements in history. In his book *The Conflict of Generations,* Feuer wrote, "The participatory democrat has no use for elections, votes, parliamentary procedures; his basic argument is that since the masses are nonparticipant, the elite actually must act on their behalf." This was Leninism: "Lenin's theory of action by a small, dictatorial elite translated into the language of the nonviolent movement."

The "New Left" of the 1960's, as represented by *Port Huron,* broke with the "Old Left," which had tied its fortunes to the Soviet Union and the Comintern, the world Communist movement. The 1939 Nazi-Soviet Pact discredited America's Old Left and shamed any intellectuals who believed in Moscow's idealism; Khrushchev's 1956 revelations of Stalin's crimes stripped the few remaining Old Left supporters of any credibility or sympathy.

By contrast, the New Left seemed to offer an alternative. It proposed a genuine form of communism that owed no allegiance to a foreign power or tainted history. In this respect, SDS was an authentic product of an American brand of dialectical materialism. SDS fought its own class struggle, not Stalin's, not Khrushchev's.

As an American hybrid, the New Left developed its own model of proletarian revolution. Borrowing from the Cuban, Vietnamese and Chinese models, the New Left attempted to embody the purity of Third World revolution against industrial capitalism and bourgeois elitism. The ideological ambitions for the movement were set by such figures as the Algerian revolutionary Franz Fanon, whose *The Wretched of the Earth* (1959) explained the role of violence in liberation; the German philosopher Herbert Marcuse, whose *One Dimensional Man* (1964) analyzed the false promise of modern industrial society, and the French Marxist Regis Debray, whose *Revolution in the Revolution* (1967) was a primer for guerilla insurrection. The example of Che Guevara, the iconic "Lone Ranger" of world revolution, inspired young professors and graduate students who dreamt of social transformation; his image was on their office and dorm room walls.

From 1960 to 1964 SDS aligned itself with the civil rights movement. SDS joined with Martin Luther King, Stokely Carmichael's Student Non-violent Coordinating Committee (SNCC), the Congress of Racial Equality (CORE) and other groups in marching through the South against Jim Crow. But by early 1965 there were over 24,000 U.S. troops in South Vietnam and the SDS shifted its focus to the war. A core of radical anti-war dissidents met at Yale University in March 1965 to debate how to oppose U.S. involvement in the war, already in its third year. They decided to organize mass demonstrations.

On May 2, 1965 SDS organized a march on the U.N. by 1,000 students waving placards and attacking American "imperialism." SDS also held rallies that day in Boston, San Francisco and Madison, Wisconsin, giving birth to the May 2 Movement (M2M). SDS set America on what would become a decade-long journey of protest, confrontation and demonstration.

The protests soon turned ugly. From the start some SDS members solicited support for the enemy. Haverford College student Russell Stetler collected money for medical supplies for the National Liberation Front, Vietnam's communist revolutionaries. Stetler's willingness to identify with the Communist enemy reflected what quickly became the most troubling aspect of SDS: it was infiltrated by members or ex-members of the Communist Party.

For instance, in 1962 "ultra-leftists" who had quit or been purged by the Communist Party, USA (CPUSA) formed the Progressive Labor Party (PLP). PLP and SDS became close allies. They opposed the Vietnam War, not because they thought it was *against* America's national interest, but because they believed the Vietnam War *represented* America's corrupt values and corporate interests.

PLP soon dominated SDS and the May 2 Movement. Progressive Labor chairman Milton Rosen, a former Communist Party member, was the party's chief "theoretician." Fred Jerome, son of the head of the CPUSA cultural division, was PLP publications editor, while PLP Harlem chairman William Epton came from the Young Communist League. Professing a Marxist-Leninist-Maoist ideology, the party was organized into a tight, centralized bureaucracy reminiscent of Lenin's concept of the "cell." It required complete dedication to a permanent "class struggle."

PLP and SDS rejected the U.S. government's reasons for intervening in Vietnam—to defend a democratic South Vietnam and halt the advance of Communism. Their own explanation was Marxist to the core: America's ruling corporate elite sought a neocolonial empire to fill the vacuum left by France's withdrawal from Indochina. It was the responsibility of radicals to take action necessary to overcome a hopelessly corrupt and reactionary U.S. ruling class. Their strategy: keep society's "power structure" in a continuous state of crisis and administer constant shocks to the "system."

The tactic was first used at UC Berkeley in fall 1964. SDS attempted to control the campus or paralyze it by confronting the authorities, including city and state police and, eventually, the California Army National Guard. Radicals called the liberal university a symbol of the "corporate state" and denounced university defense research that depended on Pentagon contracts.

Their leader was Mario Savio, who in 1964 launched the University of California, Berkeley Free Speech Movement. Savio once confided: "I'm tired of reading history. I want to make it."

Savio proposed to build a new society by tearing the old one down:

The conception bureaucrats have is that history has in fact come to an end. No event can occur now that the Second World is over which can change American society substantially. We proceed by standard procedure... America is becoming ever more the utopia of sterilized, automated contentment... This chrome-plated consumers' paradise would have us grow up to be well-behaved children. But an important minority of men and women coming to the front today have shown that they will die rather than be standardized, replaceable and irrelevant.

The student demonstrators called themselves the Free Speech Movement because the immediate issue was where they could gather to protest. But the campus was soon paralyzed as student "sit-ins" halted classroom activities. Eventually over 800 students were arrested (and 600 subsequently indicted) after police attempted to eject students from the Berkeley administration building.

SDS had created a radical student movement by linking student grievances at Berkeley—and at hundreds of other campuses—to what was happening 12,000 miles away in the jungles of Vietnam. Soon student protestors were demonstrating by the hundreds of thousands. They were shouting, "Hell no! We won't go," burning their draft cards, and blocking troop trains from moving.

Anti-War Firestorm

In early 1965 the Johnson Administration increased its troop deployments to South Vietnam and began a campaign of bombing North Vietnam. This was the first in a series of war "escalations" that went on for over seven years. Protesters poured into the streets, led by SDS and other Marxist groups as well as by old-line pacifists and anti-war liberals. Vietnam united the peace movement.

In Washington Dagmar Wilson led a coalition of feminist groups, including Women Strike for Peace (WSP), which called for an immediate withdrawal from Vietnam. On March 16, 1965, Alice Herz, an 82-year old Holocaust survivor and WSP member in Detroit, set herself on fire to protest the war, just as Buddhist monks had done in Vietnam. The Catholic priests Daniel and Philip Berrigan launched the first of their many publicity stunts against the war. They poured their own blood on draft records in Baltimore in 1967. A year later they burned draft records in Catonsville, Maryland. Later they would attempt to disrupt the launch of nuclear submarines and break into defense plants to symbolically disarm missile components.

As the war escalated so did the protests. In April 1965, SDS and Communist organizations like PLP, the Socialist Workers Party and the Young Socialist Alliance organized 25,000 to protest the war in Washington, D.C.—at that time the largest demonstration against an existing war in U.S. history. One month later, 18,000 people attended a SANE rally in Madison Square Garden to hear baby doctor Benjamin Spock and others denounce "Johnson's War."

New groups seized the anti-war initiative. The Vietnam Day Committee, led by Jerry Rubin, urged U.S. recognition of the Vietnamese communist National Liberation Front and the impeachment of President Johnson. Rubin's followers gave

124

soldiers leaflets attacking "this nightmare war" and clustered on train tracks to interrupt troop departures from the Oakland, California embarkation center.

Anti-war agitation reached a crescendo in the last years of the 1960's as the war reverted to conventional "search and destroy" ground operations accompanied by massive air strikes. Overall, between 1965 and 1970 it is estimated that four million people in 560 groups joined organized anti-war protests.

The largest umbrella organization was called the National Coordinating Committee to End the War in Vietnam (NCCEWV). It helped the anti-war movement maintain a degree of unity and coordination despite the proliferating groups. Still, there were profound divisions between Old and New Leftists, radicals and liberals, religious pacifists and political activists, violent revolutionaries and advocates of nonviolence. Only a common hostility to the Johnson and Nixon administrations overcame their differences over tactics and aims.

The divisions were immediately apparent. For instance, SDS planned the April 1965 protest rally by calling for "non-exclusionary" sponsorship. This was a code word inviting the participation of Communist organizations like the Maoists of the PLP. SDS overcame the opposition of SANE and other more centrist and pacifist groups.

Communists played the decisive role in influencing radical protests against the Vietnam War. Historian Adam Garfinkle has written, "Marxist influence was not apparent to most... in part because it was deliberately concealed in order to maximize the size and power of the evolving public protest." Only when the war widened did the influence of the extreme left on the protest movement become increasingly apparent.

The sad truth is that the war protesters believed their enemy was the United States. As SDS president Paul Potter told the April 1965 rally:

The further we explore the reality of what this country is doing ... in Vietnam we are driven to the conclusion... that the United States may well be the greatest threat to peace in the world today... We must name the system. We must name it, describe it, analyze it, understand it and change it. For it is only when that system is changed... that there can be any hope for stopping the forces that create a war in South Vietnam.

"Hell NO! We Won't Go!"

Anti-war rallies grew ever larger. In March 1966, the Fifth Avenue Peace Parade Committee, a coalition group led by the country's leading pacifist, A.J. Muste, was able to muster 50,000 demonstrators in New York and 150,000 overseas to protest the war.

Anti-war protest grew more outrageous. Protesters began to burn their draft cards and then burned the American flag. Some made pilgrimages to Hanoi, the enemy capital. Most Americans remember these visits as the most visible and contemptible legacy of the anti-war movement.

One particularly bitter memory is of actress Jane Fonda sitting in the seat of a North Vietnamese anti-aircraft gun wearing a field helmet in mock combat against American aircraft. "Hanoi Jane" was preceded by a 1965 Hanoi trip led by historian and Communist party member Herbert Aptheker. He was accompanied by SDS leader Tom Hayden (Fonda married him in 1973) and historian Staughton Lynd. They began a steady stream of sojourns to the totalitarian "host," which often featured a meeting with North Vietnam president Ho Chi Minh and carefully staged declarations against the United States.

As the war intensified, the peace movement began building ties to civil rights leaders like Martin Luther King and to young black radicals like Stokeley Carmichael and H. "Rap" Brown. Carmichael and Brown began their political careers committed to Dr. King's creed of nonviolence but ended them by supporting the Black Panther Party, an advocate for armed struggle. Ironically, the anti-war movement's efforts at coalition-building weakened their public support. Americans did not strongly support the Vietnam war, but they distrusted a peace movement that seemed to deliberately provoke domestic social unrest. Anti-war groups suffered when their cause was linked in the public mind to angry black protests such as those that erupted into 150 inner-city race riots after Dr. King's assassination on April 4, 1968.

The massive North Vietnamese "Tet Offensive" in January 1968 demoralized those who hoped the war could be won. Another irony: it increased public opposition to anti-war groups. The country was polarized. *Time* magazine labeled the anti-war street rebels as "Vietniks" and "Peaceniks" who were alienated from the vast geographic and psychological locale known as "Middle America."

Between 1967 and 1970 the anti-war movement reached its apogee. An October 1967 "March on the Pentagon" attracted over 100,000 protesters. In the first half of 1968 more than 200 demonstrations rocked university campuses. Incoming President Richard Nixon and Henry Kissinger, his national security advisor, ended the draft, attempted to "Vietnamize" the war, and promised an "end in sight." But their attempt to mix and match military with diplomatic initiatives only fed the fires of protest.

As the war went on the New Left grew increasingly violent. The national psychosis was on full display when Dr. Benjamin Spock, who had nurtured generations of mothers and babies, was indicted by a federal grand jury for aiding draft dodgers. Dominated by SDS fringe groups such as the violent "Weathermen"—whose name comes from the lyrics of a Bob Dylan song, "Subterranean Homesick Blues" (*"You don't need a weatherman to know which way the wind blows"*)—the anti-war movement became a threat to civil order. The Weathermen called for "the destruction of U.S. imperialism and the achievement of a classless world: world communism." SDS had over 300 local chapters, which were infiltrated by militant Communist and socialist revolutionaries. Didactic SDS slogans urged "the need for armed struggle as the only road to revolution." And the protesters chanted, "The whole world is watching" when police fought with them outside the 1968 Democratic Convention in Chicago.

By the summer of 1969 new anti-war mobilization committees were preparing to force the Nixon Administration to withdraw from Vietnam. Anti-war Democrats who opposed the Johnson Administration and supported his challengers, Senators Eugene McCarthy (D-MN) and Robert Kennedy (D-NY), joined the radicals. McCarthy supporter Sam Brown led the "Vietnam Moratorium Committee," which became the nerve center for an effort to "suspend business" for a giant October 15 demonstration. A rival "New Mobilization Committee to End the War in Vietnam" (the "New Mobe") planned demonstrations for mid-November. The New Mobe combined Old Left activists with Trotskyites and younger radical pacifists. It was led by David Dellinger and Rennie Davis, both members of the Chicago Seven,

127

and later by Sidney Peck, an unindicted co-conspirator. Despite some tension, the two umbrella groups supervised the largest mass demonstrations in American history.

The largest was the October 15, 1969 Moratorium. An estimated one million people took part in nationwide demonstrations, many of these in cities and towns with no prior history of protest. Earlier protests had featured counter-culture rock and folk singers like Joan Baez, Bob Dylan, and Peter, Paul and Mary. But the Moratorium reflected the widening opposition to the war.

The appearance at the Washington demonstration of banjo player Earl Scruggs, a bluegrass music icon, symbolized the broadening of support for the peace movement. Bluegrass was associated with southern patriotism. But when Scruggs and his son Randy walked on stage the movement broke new ground. Scruggs later told reporters, "I think the people in the South is just as concerned as the people that's walkin' the streets here today. I'm sincere about bringin' our boys back home. I'm disgusted and in sorrow about the boys that we've lost over there. And if I could see a good reason to continue, I wouldn't be here today."

John Kerry and the "Days of Rage"

Just as the anti-Vietnam war movement seemed on the verge of unity, the old factionalism emerged. Ideological splits divided protesters into bitter parts and the most violent factions gained the upper hand. After the massive October 15 demonstrations, protests were scheduled for mid-November, 1969. They drew over 350,000 protesters to San Francisco and 500,000 to Washington. But soon the members of SDS most prone to acts of revolutionary violence, the hyper-radical Weather Underground, steered the course of protest.

The Weathermen promised to "bring the war home," in the words of one pamphlet. That meant violence. Between September 1969 and May 1970 there were more than 250 anti-war bombings, most of them attributed to the Weather Underground. Banks and corporate headquarters were favorite targets. SDS announced "Days of Rage" in 1969 as student strikes and administration closures hit over 500 colleges and universities during the 1969-

1970 academic year, none so notorious as at Ohio's Kent State University, where National Guardsmen shot and killed four students on May 4, 1970 during protests against the Nixon Administration's "incursion" into Cambodia. The nation appeared on the verge of anarchy.

During 1970 there were 423 reported attacks on police stations and 101 against military posts. Many of these were attributed to the Black Panthers. Dissidents and draft protesters organized groups with names like "The Resistance" and "Resist." Americans even began hearing from returning Vietnam veterans, whose testimony provided the most lasting echoes of the anti-war generation.

In 1970 Vietnam Veterans Against the War (VVAW) initiated what was described at the time as "a mixture of peace march, mobile speak-out and guerrilla theatre." Clad in battle fatigues, many on crutches or in wheelchairs, veterans offered accounts of their first-hand experiences to protest the war. VVAW and other veterans' protest groups, including the American Servicemen's Union and the Concerned Officer's Movement, organized a "spring offensive" that aimed to force Congress to cut off war funding and move toward domestic reform. Veterans spoke out against atrocities, real and alleged, including the infamous My Lai massacre, and collectively threw their medals and ribbons away in highly publicized attempts to attract media attention. Many veterans participated in an April 24, 1971 demonstration in Washington, which brought over 300,000 protesters to the Capitol.

On April 22, 1971 one VVAW member named John F. Kerry testified before the Senate Foreign Relations Committee. The following year he would run unsuccessfully for the U.S. House of Representatives. But Kerry's political career actually began that day in front of the Committee and in full view of TV cameras. Kerry's indictment of his country and fellow soldiers in the field remains a lasting link between his generation then and the one now protesting America's war against international terrorism.

America's role in Vietnam, according the 2004 Democratic presidential nominee, was anything but honorable. Kerry's accusations covered both civilian and military leaders:

Where is the leadership? We are here to ask where are McNamara, Rostow, Bundy, Gilpatric, and so many others. Where are they now that we, the men whom they sent off to war, have returned?

These are commanders who have deserted their troops, and there is no more serious crime in the law of war .The Army says they never leave their wounded. The Marines say they never leave even their dead. These men have left all the casualties and retreated behind a pious shield of public rectitude.

But Kerry's chief complaint was the American soldier, whom he charged with deliberate and sustained atrocities. Relating stories he had discussed with other veterans, Kerry depicted American soldiers in Vietnam as vicious and savage:

[Veterans] testified to war crimes committed in Southeast Asia, not isolated incidents but crimes committed on a day-to-day basis with the full awareness of officers at all levels of command...They told stories at times they had personally raped, cut off ears, cut off heads, taped wires from portable telephones to human genitals and turned up the power, cut off limbs, blown up bodies, randomly shot at civilians, razed villages in fashion reminiscent of Genghis Khan, shot cattle and dogs for fun, poisoned food stocks, and generally ravaged the countryside of South Vietnam in addition to the normal ravage of war, and the normal and very particular ravaging which is done by the applied bombing power of this country.

The legacy of Vietnam that Kerry describes is terrifying, far removed from academic revisionist histories. It tore the heart out of the American character. As we have seen throughout the 2004 presidential campaign, these words came back to haunt candidate Kerry because they brought Vietnam and the near-forgotten protests against the war back into our current politics. They revive bitter memories. But they also focus America's attention on the current anti-war movement, whose ominous future is before us.

After Vietnam

Vietnam is America's only "lost" war. It was not lost on the battlefield—the testimony of top North Vietnamese generals confirms that U.S. forces won every major battlefield encounter—but at home in the "minds and hearts" of Americans. What role did anti-war demonstrations play in determining the final outcome?

Adam Garfinkle's 1995 book, *Telltale Hearts*, challenges the view, shared by both dissidents and Vietnam war supporters, that the anti-war movement determined the war's outcome. Garfinkle, a former editor of *The National Interest*, concludes:

The antiwar movement neither lost the war nor caused the subsequent bloodbath in Southeast Asia. In the broadest sense, the war was lost because the American ship of state had lost its bearings... the war was not won because U.S. administrative, diplomatic and especially military strategies failed... None of these sources of American defeat was set in motion or significantly worsened either by antiwar activism or by fear of it in Washington.

Whatever its impact on the Vietnam War's outcome, the anti-war movement certainly has had a profound and continuing impact on American society and culture. "What did you do in the war?" is a question no political candidate of a certain age escapes. The current anti-war movement looks to its predecessor for guidance and inspiration, especially since many leaders of current groups helped pull the strings 35 years ago. Indeed, the word "quagmire," as it was used in Vietnam, has become a term of art, a synonym for defeatism in Iraq.

It is instructive to look at how two architects of the Cold War saw Vietnam era protest. Henry A. Kissinger and George F. Kennan were the archetypal scholar/diplomats of their generation. They differed on the conduct of the Vietnam War, but their assessments of the anti-war movement complement each another.

Kissinger saw Vietnam protest directed against his own policies and he understood the cultural, generational and ideological chasm separating the movement from him:

The leaders of the Peace Movement considered the war so repugnant that an honorable extrication from Vietnam had come to sound like an absurdity. What the Nixon Administration had perceived as potential national humiliation, the Vietnam protesters treated as a desirable national catharsis. The Administration sought an outcome that would enable America to continue its postwar international role as the protector and sustainer of free peoples—precisely the role that many in the Peace Movement wanted to end, viewing it as the arrogance and presumption of a flawed society.

131

Kennan opposed the Johnson and Nixon Administration's conduct of the Vietnam War, but he did not join the peace movement. His position, delivered in testimony before Congress and in print, urged political prudence ("realism") and geopolitical restraint. The peace movement was indifferent to Kennan's concerns. To him, the anti-war movement was anti-democratic:

> These people also pose a problem in the quality of their citizenship. One thing they all seem to have in common - the angry ones as well as the quiet ones—is a complete rejection of, or indifference to, the political system of this country. The quiet ones turn their backs upon it, as though it did not concern them. The angry ones reject it by implication, insofar as they refuse to recognize the validity of its workings or to respect the discipline which, as a system of authority, it unavoidably entails.

At the heart of the anti-war movement's opposition to the Vietnam War is a counter-cultural opposition to America's political culture. This "culture war" over Vietnam was at its most intense for almost a decade, and it has never ceased. "Vietnam" is a metaphor: something to be forgotten or a warning of things to come. It haunts debate over Iraq, as it did the 2004 presidential campaign.

A new opposition to the War Against Terror and the occupation of Iraq arises today, seemingly from the ashes of the old protest movement. The trouble with this analogy is that the fire never went out; it only is being rekindled. The causes and many of the players remain the same.

Compare the current anti-war movement to its counterpart during the Vietnam War. United for Peace and Justice was the principal organizer of protest during the 2004 Republican Convention. In 1971 the House Committee on Internal Security investigated an anti-war group with a nearly identical name: People's Coalition for Peace and Justice (PCPJ). The similarity is not coincidental.

Subcommittee Chairman Richard Ichord (D-MO) opened the 1971 hearing by noting that "In the initial hearing last month, the committee received considerable documentary evidence and testimony establishing the significant presence of the Communist Party, U.S.A., in PCPJ and of the Trotskyite communist Socialist Workers Party (SWP) and its youth arm, the Young Socialist

Alliance" (YSA). Chairman Ichord further noted, "There is a general lack of knowledge about the communist nature of the SWP and YSA." Ichord's observation still stands, as does the committee's overall finding that communists and other professional radical organizers dominate the peace movement.

Another link to the past is the use of "peace" as a subterfuge for promoting other social and political causes. Subcommittee witness William T. Poole had testified that peace reform was a tactic to overhaul America's social order: "They are concentrating not just on promoting withdrawal of American forces from Indochina, but they are concentrating on what they regard as the related issues of poverty and repression..."

Poole submitted for the record a statement from PCPJ on the real nature of the organization:

The People's Coalition is committed to a multi-issue and multi-tactical approach, linking the struggle for peace in Indochina with the struggle for radical change in America, using nonviolent direct action, people's lobbying, and resistance.

Another witness, Herbert Romerstein, submitted a recording of remarks coming from a PCPJ sound truck at an April 24, 1971 mass rally sponsored by the New Mobilization (New Mobe), the anti-war umbrella organization:

The People's Coalition is made up of groups that used to participate in the New Mobilization Committee and, in addition, other peace groups, black liberation groups, Puerto Rican liberation groups, Chicano groups, Welfare Rights, SCLC, and different groups we work with. So, if you'd like information on this coalition, the People's Coalition, this is the second big demonstration that we've sponsored. We had one before at Wall Street, which was part of the war against repression and a tribute in action for Dr. Martin Luther King. If you are interested in the struggles against war, racism and repression and agree with us that you have to unite those struggles and unite the people struggling against them in order to win at all those things, then please come over and get information from us.

Romerstein expanded on this point by referring to the tactic of the "front" group, which was used by the Vietnamese Communist Party:

One of the things that I would like to raise is the basic communist concept of work with other people and other organizations and as to why the communists engage in united front or common front activities. General Vo Nguyen Giap has written a book called "People's War, People's Army," where... he explains what he called the 'policy of front,' and that is to neutralize part of the enemy, the wavering elements among the enemy, to neutralize all those who could be neutralized and to divide all those who could be divided.

Another document from over thirty years ago reminds us that the enemy benefits when there is war resistance on the American homefront. On May 12, 1971, Nguyen Minh Vy, a deputy minister of North Vietnam's apparatus in Paris, told an American peace activist how Hanoi viewed the protest movement:

I would like to say that we felt that the Spring offensive of the American anti war movement was a great success. We followed very closely the hourly reports of the arrests in Washington... It is hard to find the words to express our feelings. We realize how difficult the struggle was. We would greatly appreciate a continuation of anti war activities throughout the summer.

The current statements issued by ANSWER, United for Peace and Justice, and Not In Our Name indicate that the aims, tactics and targets of the modern peace movement are unchanged. Today, however, there is no congressional oversight for such groups even as America undertakes its greatest fight against terror. Post-Watergate congressional "reform" in the 1970s crippled the CIA and other overseas intelligence agencies, and it destroyed the U.S. government's capacity for domestic surveillance. The House Internal Security Committee was abolished in 1975. Three years after September 11, 2001, there still is nothing to replace it.

Chapter 6

FINAL REFLECTIONS

It is generally agreed that World War I, more than any other event, transformed the politics of modern history. Among its other legacies, World War I elevated the major revolutionary moments—communism, fascism, socialism, democratic liberalism—all of which would challenge traditional authority and promise a new millennium. Utopia never arrived, but its pursuit destroyed more nations and killed more civilians and soldiers in the twentieth century than any comparable time in world history.

The radicalization of peace activism is another major consequence of the "Great War" and is a direct result of the carnage of the time. In his study of the twentieth century peace movement, Lawrence S. Wittner noted the effect on Americans produced by trench warfare on the Western front: "The pacifist ideal, while possessed of a long and distinguished history, never took hold in the United States until the aftermath of World War I, when a wave of disillusionment with that conflict swept across the country."

International politics continues to owe much to the Great War. Writing thirty-five years ago, historian John Lukacs described a world still immersed in Cold War politics and nuclear threats, but one that is still very familiar:

The War of 1914 beat the stuffing out of the bourgeois. Not only revolutionary ideas but radical new forms of manners, of art, of fashion, of entertainment, of publicity became commonplace, especially in the great capitals of the Western world. The Americanization of Europe, indeed, of

135

much of the world, was in full swing. Not only was the United States the richest country in the world, entire governments depending on its financial decisions; now there were millions of people in Europe who knew the names of Hollywood film stars while they knew not the name of their own prime minister. American music, American movies, American techniques of production and of publicity were emulated everywhere. The revolutionary enemies of the bourgeois order were not exempt from these inclinations.

Of course, the origins of the peace movement pre-date 1914, as has been explained here. But the "revolutionary enemies of the bourgeois" are still among us, and their number includes the radicals who dominate the anti-war movement.

How, then, shall we assess the Peace Movement in its many guises? Several conclusions emerge from this study.

The first is failure. The failure of pacifism, old and new. The failure of reform, of socialism, of democracy, of internationalism, of isolationism, of utopianism and, lastly, the failure of communism. These ideas and the institutions embodying them, taken singly or together, have failed to overcome the propensity of nations and peoples to engage in almost constant warfare. What was true in the seventeenth century remains true today. War continues to claim victims in Iraq, and in all corners of the globe, on a yearly, monthly and daily basis.

A 1989 study found that there had been 136 wars since the end of World War II, mostly intra-state or regional, and they had taken over 21 million people to the grave. That was 15 years ago. What would a study in 2005 reveal? The appalling answer: millions more dead. The statistics offer no clue as to what causes war or how to bring peace. When we reach such appalling levels statistics can do little more than numb the mind and soul. In Rwanda in 1994, over 800,000 civilians were clubbed, shot or stabbed to death in a span of months. That is just one "statistic." Such references only demonstrate war's near-endless and tragic repetition without regard to time or circumstance. The reasons for war change, but the *institution* of war does not.

After centuries of systematic and sustained failure what can be expected of organized movements for peace? The glaring answer provides little comfort to sincere pacifists of any political stripe.

This suggests a second finding of this study.

The triumph of ideology over ideas is surely central to politics in the twentieth century. This is true of anti-war politics, as the first chapters of this study indicate. Ideology has overwhelmed the politics of the modern peace movement, which has become a movement of "the Left"

The political philosopher George Sabine observed that ideology provides group cohesion, identity and continued meaning:

The word "ideology is the only term from Marx's formidable vocabulary that has come into common use, and though Marx did not coin the word, he gave it more or less the meaning that it now has in common usage. The word has long ceased to have any connotation of Marxism. Its meaning hardly admits of precise definition, though it refers to a fact now generally recognized. This is the fact that any social group which acts together as a unit must have a common body of beliefs, values and convictions that "reflects" its understanding of itself, of its environment, and of other social groups with which it has transactions. Such a body of common beliefs is indeed a condition of its existence as a group.

But if ideology has kept America's peace movement alive, it has not kept it well. The ideology of the modern peace movement has kept peace advocacy far from the center of politics. Peace activists can irritate, infuriate, enrage and engage, but by themselves they cannot further their own political ambitions let alone create conditions for international peace. Anti-war groups may be self-sustaining, but they are not effective engines of change. As always, peace is a condition made possible by the foreign and national security policies of governments and nations.

The failure of the contemporary peace movement troubles many anti-war activists who complain that the far-left groups dominating the movement are discrediting peace advocacy. Georgetown University historian Michael Kazin reports that the American left is "sharply divided" about its leaders. "The organizers of the recent Washington and San Francisco marches," he said, "refuse to say anything critical of Saddam Hussein." Writing in *Liberty* magazine, professor Stephen Cox echoes his point: "More clearly than ever before, I believe, the great liability of the anti-war movement is... the anti-war movement. It is a movement that programmatically refuses to separate itself from radical left sentiment."

Some believe the hard-left that controls the anti-war movement needs allies to give it political "cover" to get beyond its self-imposed political corner. Writing in Patrick Buchanan's magazine *The American Conservative*, British socialist Neil Clark offered just such a proposition by suggesting an international left-right alliance against Bush Administration policies: "Until the Left is ready in its hordes to link up electorally with the old antiwar Right, the brutal truth is that we have no chance of defeating the Bush/Blair axis."

Such combinations are not unknown to history—witness the positions of Robert Taft and Henry Wallace immediately after World War II. However, their failure to provide a coherent alternative to President Truman's policy of containment suggests that any modern left/right coalition is most unlikely.

Here's another conclusion that can be derived from this study: The peace movement fails even when it seems to have achieved its own purposes. That's the lesson of the period between the two world wars. Such successes as internationalism and anti-militarism achieved in the 1920's and 1930's contained the seeds of their own failure. Pearl Harbor was a definitive refutation of the policies of legal/moral utopianism and isolationism.

After Pearl Harbor, the U.S. government turned against its past peace policies. American soldiers in the millions were sent overseas and defense budgets skyrocketed. In reaction, peace organizations turned against patriotism and swung sharply to the left, where they remain, noisy, annoying but largely ineffective. Any improvement in the movement's prospects is more likely to be the consequence of inept government policies than the result of movement strategies produced in a vacuum.

Our survey of the history of anti-war resistance shows that activists can change national security policies, but only in temporary and superficial ways. Whatever successes the peace movement has claimed were either transitory illusions of permanent peace or a reaction leading to an equally delusional isolationism. Eventually, power politics has destroyed the best creations of pacifists or ideologically-driven activists. Even during the Vietnam War, at the height of the "movement," the power of the anti-war opposition only reflected the successes or failures of government policies. The anti-war movement grew as the war continued year-after-year without achieving its ends. Had the Johnson Administration won the war in 1967 there would have been little or no authoritative anti-war opposition. Successful wars destroy the very roots of anti-war movements.

The U.S. government's war on terror, and, in particular, its occupation of Iraq will test the current protest movement. If the policies of President Bush prevail and produce success, then the peace movement will fail. But the war in Iraq is nearing its third year without conclusion, and the violence continues. If this persists we can expect protest to grow proportionally.

Chapter three demonstrated the domestic consequences of inconclusive military campaigns. It would be easy to cite other examples: the Seminole War of the 1830's, other Indian campaigns in the nineteenth century, and the American occupations of Haiti and the Dominican Republic between 1915 and 1934. Even Theodore Roosevelt, the most enthusiastic supporter of aggressive expansionism came to regret his ambition for the Philippine occupation, which he labeled the "heel of Achilles."

How will the United States mission in Iraq affect the war on terror? Will Iraq become a "heel of Achilles" in 2005 and beyond? The consequences of U.S. policy, not the actions of the protesters, will ultimately determine war and peace in the region.

But the anti-war movement is waiting off stage and we know its character. ANSWER, UPJ, NION and the rest are anticipating failure. At bottom, they welcome failure and are eager to exploit even the most cursory setbacks. Thus, the movement's effectiveness in influencing the American people will depend on how the second Bush Administration conducts the political-military campaign in Iraq.

Ironically, war resistance in America still follows the flag. We can expect this general rule of politics to govern future war protests, particularly in 2005. While President Bush's victory has been analyzed backwards and forwards, from "red" and "blue" perspectives, little attention has been given to the Bush Administration's relationship to the anti-war movement. Neither has there been much speculation on how a Kerry win would have affected war protest. This is not an idle point, as Kerry was only a few percentage points away from victory.

Kerry might be thought exempt from anti-war protest as he was once "one of them," and he also opposed the Gulf War. However, it is likely that a President Kerry taking ambiguous positions on the current occupation of Iraq would be a continuing target of protest. Kerry might make promises of withdrawing from Iraq while relying on his claim to heroism in Vietnam to give himself political cover. And certainly the prospects for a military withdrawal would be a much greater for Kerry than for Bush, whose political legitimacy depends on achieving a defined victory over the insurgents. Still, a Kerry presidency that promised an eventual withdrawal would provoke an emboldened anti-war opposition. Convinced that it could win an internal "family quarrel" within the community of the progressive Left, anti-war activists would put unrelenting pressure on the Administration. Any disappointments, as occurred during the Johnson Administration, would sour anti-war activists on the new President. So it is likely that the anti-war movement would retain its fervor even if John Kerry were elected president.

Of course the reality of the election's outcome—the shock of November 2, 2004—only promises a more strident and dedicated anti-war left organizing against the Administration. President Bush faces an intransigent foe.

The movement knows what it is up against. After November 2, United for Peace and Justice issued an appeal "to regroup and take the long view." UPJ promised, like the Democratic Party, to heed its wake-up call and search for more imaginative ways to win:

United for Peace and Justice always knew that our work to end the occupation of Iraq would not be immediately affected by the outcome of the presidential race. We are preparing to move into a period of much more focused organizing on the Iraq war, working with local groups around the country on implementing plans to reach the people we don't usually talk to. As that work unfolds, we are exploring ways to strengthen the impact of our mobilizations, including planning for activities that might make it harder for those in charge to actually carry out the war.

If this statement is representative, it actually makes UPJ a more serious opponent of the Bush Administration. It suggests that UPJ's approach will be more intelligent and attuned to political reality, less ideological and fanatical. It could produce more "strange bedfellow" political coalitions. More importantly, it could lead anti-war groups to place more emphasis on *organization*, the element that distinguishes a political movement from mere dissent.

A recent online Alternet.org article by icon Tom Hayden, "How to End the War in Iraq," (profiled by John Seward in *frontpagemag.com*, December 6, 2004) announces the essence of the anti-war movement's latest strategy: "The antiwar movement can force the Bush Administration to leave Iraq by denying it the funding, troops, and alliances necessary to its strategy for dominance." Drawing on his experience with SDS during the Vietnam War period, Hayden outlines a plan similar to the end-game of that era. First, he proposes to build grassroots pressure at the congressional district level to challenge U.S. war funding. Next, he would work closely with Democrats to make the party fully anti-war without any ambiguity. Hawkish Democrats would be marked for challenge as "collaborators." The movement would foster dissent, disobedience and desertion (the 3 D's) by military personnel, including "another underground railroad to havens in Canada for those who refuse to serve." Hayden's explains his attempt to breathe new life into the antiwar movement in a six-point summary: "In short: pinch the funding arteries, push the Democrats to become an opposition party, ally with anti-war Republicans, support dissenting soldiers, make 'Iraqization' more difficult, and build a peace coalition against the war coalition." Drastic action, certainly, but hardly unique in the history of the peace movement.

Obviously successful resolution of the Iraqi occupation will take the wind from the anti-war sails. But even the most favorable war outcome cannot permanently stop the leftist peace movement. Its history is too long and its message too mesmerizing for important parts of American society and in contemporary world politics.

The best prognosis for the U.S. war on terror is a "long, twilight struggle," as John Kennedy described the Cold War. Responsible observers understand this reality, and they understand that a vigorous and dangerous anti-war protest movement will accompany the war on terror. This book has identified the movement's tactics and strategies.

141

A free people must defend itself against enemies abroad and within. We will have to fight a protracted war on a multifaceted front. The enemies of American liberty were on the battlefield and the high seas during the American Revolution and they are there today. They also are to be found within our vulnerable but democratic homeland. "There is nothing new under the sun." *(Ecclesiastes 1:9)*

1. International A.N.S.W.E.R. (Act Now to Stop War & End Racism)

International A.N.S.W.E.R. Coalition List

Steering Committee:
IFCO/Pastors for Peace
Free Palestine Alliance - U.S.
Haiti Support Network
Partnership for Civil Justice - LDEF
Nicaragua Network
Bayan - USA/International
Korea Truth Commission
International Action Center
Muslim Student Association - National
Kensington Welfare Rights Union
Mexico Solidarity Network
Middle East Children's Alliance

Partial List of Coalition Co-Signers:
Ramsey Clark - *former U.S. Attorney General*

Bishop Thomas Gumbleton - *Auxiliary Bishop, Catholic Archdiocese of Detroit*

American Muslims for Global Peace

Al-Awda Palestine Right of Return Coalition, NY & NJ

Barbara Lubin - *Executive Director, Middle East Children's Alliance*

Rev. Lucius Walker - *Pastors for Peace*

Rev. Graylan Hagler - *Senior Minister, Plymouth Congregational Church, Washington DC*

Rev. Curtis Gatewood - *Durham, North Carolina*

Rev. Cecil Williams - *Glide Memorial Church, Washington, DC*

Robert Meeropol - *Executive Director, Rosenberg Fund for Children*

Teresa Gutierrez - *Co-Director, International Action Center, NYC*

Karen Talbot - *International Center for Peace & Justice*

Committee for a Democratic Palestine

Ismael Guadalupe - *Committee for Rescue & Development in Vieques, Puerto Rico*

Michel Chossudovsky - *Professor of Economics, University of Ottawa, Canada*

Green Party USA

Howard Zinn - *historian and author*

Michael Parenti Ph.D. - *author of 'America Besieged'*

Dick Gregory - *comedian*

David Clennon - *actor*

Ben DuPuy - *former Deputy Ambassador-at-Large, Haiti*

School Of the Americas Watch

Humdan Durrani - *President, Muslim Student Association of Richland College, Dallas, Texas*

Eric Mar - *Commissioner, San Francisco Board of Education; CFA/CTA*

Chuck Turner - *council member, Boston City Council, District 7**

Al-Awda Palestine Right of Return Coalition of New York and New Jersey

Hoshikawa Jun - *Director, Yakushima Institute, Japan*

John Gilbert - *university instructor*

Ajmal Pashtoonyar - *President, Afghan Youth Organization (AYO), St. John's, Newfoundland, Canada*

Muslims Against Racism and War

Rev. Phil Wheaton - *Committee for Indigenous Solidarity (CIS), Washington, DC*

Tom Nagy - *professor, George Washington University*

Nania Kaur Dhingra - *Sikh Student Organization, George Washington University*

Martín Espada - *poet*

Sakhi for South Asian Women

Women for Afghan Women

Stephanie Simard - *Co-president, Simmons College Feminist Union, Women's Fightback Network, Boston, Massachusetts*

Michele Naar-Obed - *Plowshares activist, Jonah House, Baltimore*

Pam Africa - *International Family & Friends of Mumia Abu-Jamal, Philadelphia, Pennsylvania*

Michel Collon – *Belgian author and journalist*

Helena Papadopoulos - *Researcher, Center for the Comparative Study of Law and Society, Rabieh, Lebanon*

Elmar Schmaehling - *Retired Admiral, German Navy, Germany*

Wolfgang Richter - *President, European Peace Forum, Germany*

Issam Makhoul - *member of the Knesset, Democratic Front for Peace and Equality (HADASH), Israel*

Sally Davies - *President, AFSCME Council 92*

Craig Newman - *Executive Board, AFSCME Local 1072*

Andre Powell - *Executive Board, AFSCME Local 112*

Eric Easton - *Vice President, National Action Network, Baltimore, Maryland*

Rev. David Carl Olson - *Community Church of Boston, Boston, Massachusetts*

Baltimore Coalition Against the War, Maryland

Women's International League for Peace and Freedom, Baltimore and Cantonsville Chapters, Maryland

Ricardo Juarez - *Pasamontañas*

Nino Pasti Foundation, Rome, Italy

Tobias Pflueger & Claudia Haydt - *Information-Post on Militarism, Germany*

New Communist Party of the Netherlands

African Immigrant and Refugee Coalition of North America

Dominican Workers Party, NYC

Chuck Kaufman - *National Co-Coordinator, Nicaragua Network*

NISGUA - *the Network in Solidarity with the People of Guatamala*

Ray LaForest - *Labor Organizer, District Council 1707 AFSCME, NYC*

Heidi Boghosian - *Executive Director, National Lawyers Guild*

Tom Hansen - *Mexico Solidarity Network, Washington, DC*

Kriss Worthington - *Berkeley City Council, Berkeley, California*

Leonora Foerstal - *Women for Mutual Security*

Asha A. Samad - *Human Rights Center*

April 25 Movement of the Dominican Republic

Njeri Shakur - *Texas Death Penalty Abolition Movement*

Michel Shehadeh - *Los Angeles 8 Case Respondent, Los Angeles, California*

Muslim Student & Faculty Association

Emmanunel M. Hizon - *Coordinator, Student Power movement, Quezon City, Manila, Philippines*

Saad Kadhim - *West Harlem Coalition, New York City*

Leslie Feinberg - *transgender author and Co-Founder, Rainbow Flags for Mumia*

Kadouri Al Kaysi - *Committee in Support of Iraqi People, New York City*

Aisha Sabadia - *Muslim Student Union, Amnesty, Ann Arbor, Michigan*

Minnie Bruce Pratt - *writer and anti-racist activist*

Vieques Support Campaign, NYC

All Peoples Congress, Baltimore, Maryland

Unity for Action, Baltimore, Maryland

Sharon Ceci - *Shop Steward, UFCW Local 27, Baltimore, Maryland*

Mitchel Cohen - *Green Party USA and Brooklyn Greens, Brooklyn*

Milos Raickovich - *College of Staten Island, CUNY*

Carlos Eden - *Raweshrar Project for Indigenous People, Chile*

Jamie York - *Cuba Advocate Newsletter, Montana*

Brian Barraza - *Association of Mexican Workers, NYC*

Justin Vitiello - *professor, Temple University, Philadelphia*

John Kim - *Veterans for Peace, NYC Chapter, NYC*

Mahtowin Munro & Moonanum James - *United American Indians of New England*

SAFRAD Somali Association

Monica Moorehead - *Workers World Party*

Arab Cause Solidarity Committee, Madrid, Spain

Congress for Korean Reunification

Struggle Against War Coalition, Italy

Trades Union International of Building and Wood Workers, Finland

LEF Foundation, St. Helena, California

Vanguard Public Foundation, San Francisco, California

Consuela Lee - *musician*

Bohemian Grove Action Network, Sonoma County, California

Sonoma County Free Press, California

Susan E. Davis - *co-chair, New York Local, National Writers Union, UAW Local 1981, NYC*

James Lafferty - *National Lawyers Guild, Los Angeles*

Campaign Against Racism & War, Oberlin, Ohio

Vietnam Veterans Against the War Anti-Imperialist

Dr. Pol De Vos - *President, Anti-Imperialist League, Belgium*

Refuse and Resist

Dr. Bert De Belder - *Coordinator, Third World Medical Aid, Belgium*

Dr. Jean Pestieau - *professor, Catholic University of Louvain, Belgium*

Tri-Valley Communities Against a Radioactive Environment, California

California Prison Focus

Anuradha Mittal - *Executive Director, Food First/Institute for Food and Development Policy*

Sandra Robertson - *Georgia Citizens Coalition on Hunger*

Al-Awda Palestine Right of Return Coalition of Massachusetts

Radio Arabiyat, Boston, Massachusetts

Vanessa Marques - *Portuguese-American Relief for Palestine*

Rima Anabtawi - *Al-Awda Palestine Right of Return Coordinating Committee*

Committee to Defend Amer Jubran and
   Palestinian Free Speech Rights

Atlanta Masjid of Al-Islam, Atlanta, Georgia

Masjid Al Muminun, Atlanta, Georgia

Hadayai Majeed - *Muslim Women's Political Action Committee*

Gloria La Riva - *International Action Center, San Francisco*

Julia Yonetani - *researcher, University of the Ryukyus, Okinawa*

Eliseo Ramírez - *Director Política, Internacional de Voz
   Proletaria, Buenos Aires, Argentina*

Ali Baghdadi - *editor, Arab Journal, Woodridge, Illinois*

Claire Alby - *documentary filmmaker, Paris, France*

Gil Ben Aych - *philosopher and writer, Paris, France*

Debbie Anderson - *founder, The Rosa Luxemburg Collective,
   McDonough, New York*

Prof. Peter Erlinder - *professor of law and former president,
   National Lawyers Guild, St. Paul, Minnesota*

Yafar Gonzalez Bornez - *Madrasa Islamica Imam Ar-Rida (A.S.)
   - UMMAH, Granada, España*

Abigal Coburn - *student, Friends World Program, Southampton,
   New York*

Ian Harvey - *Florida Education Association, AFL-CIO, Naples,
   Florida*

Kevin Ramirez - *Central Committee for Conscientious Objectors,
   Philadelphia, Pennsylvania*

Richard Hugus - *Cape Cod Coalition Against Iraq Sanctions,
   Falmouth, Massachusetts*

Sergio Sánchez - *Facultad de Ingeniería, Universidad Central de
   Venezuela, Utopía Universitaria, Caracas, Venezuela*

Vera Vratusa-Zunjic - *Department of Sociology, Beograd,
   Yugoslavia*

Steven Gillis - *Executive Board, USWA local 8751,
   Boston School Bus Drivers, Boston, Massachusetts*

Gerry Scoppettuolo - *Director of Education, South New
   Hampshire HIV/AIDS Task Force*

Keith McHenry - *co-founder, Food Not Bombs, Tucson, Arizona*

Teresa and Blase Bonpane - *Office of the Americas, Los Angeles, California*

Mohau Pheko - *Pan Africanist Women's Organisation of Azania, Johannesburg, South Africa*

Seena Yacoob - *Researcher, Johannesburg, Gauteng, South Africa*

Evangelos Mahairas - *Honorary President, World Peace Council, Greece*

Mark Taylor - *professor, Princeton Theological Seminary, Educators for Mumia*

David Sole - *President, UAW Local 2334, Detroit, Michigan*

Nadine Rosa-Rosso - *General Secretary, Workers' Party of Belgium, Belgium*

Stan Goff - *writer and organizer, North Carolina Network for Popular Democracy*

Sidney J. Gluck - *Chairman, US-China Society of Friends*

Veronica Golos - *poet, NYC*

David Obiekwe Quarter - *Toronto, Canada*

Richard Roper - *England*

Mark Burwinkel - *Cincinnati, Ohio*

Lee Mager - *London, England*

Heather Cottin - *Long Island, New York*

Beatriz Morales - *Madrid, Spain*

Campaign Against Plan Colombia, Barcelona, Spain

Garibaldi Collective, Barcelona, Spain

Batasana, Euskal, Basque Country

Karim Lopez - *Institute for Mass Communications*

Oklahoma Socialist Cooperative, Oklahoma Radical Women

Freedom Socialist Party

Johnnie Stevens - *People's Video Network, NYC*

Arab Women's Solidarity Association, San Francisco Chapter, San Francisco

Savas Michael-Matsas - *General Secretary, Christian Rakovsky Balkan Socialist Center, Athens, Greece*

A Jewish Voice for Peace, San Francisco

Marco Frucht - *Editor and Publisher, Activist Times, Green Bay, Wisconsin*

Greg Miaskiewicz - *Adams County Green Party, Gettysburg, Pennsylvania*

G.N. Saibaba - *general secretary, AIPRF, India*

Klaus von Raussendorff - *Anti-Imperialistische Korrespondenz, Bonn, Germany*

Arab Cause Solidarity Committee, Spain

Mimi Adams - *Arab-Jewish Dialog, Albuquerque*

Gavan McCormack - *Australian National University, Canberra*

Bay Area CISPES, San Francisco

Bündnis Global Gegen Krieg (Global Alliance Against War), From, Germany

Saundra McMillan - *professor, California State University at Long Beach*

Jason Johnston - *Campaign Against Racism and War, Oberlin, Ohio*

Campaña Contra Plan Colombia (Campaign Against Plan Colombia)

Robert Franck - *professor, Catholic University of Louvain, Belgium*

Michael Green - *Ex Dir., Center for Environmental Health, San Francisco*

Aton Ra - *Center of Strategic Future, Stockholm, Stockholm, Sweden*

College Voice

Roy Rollin - *College Voice, NYC*

Committee on US-Latin American Relations (CUSLAR), Ithaca, New York

Manfred Eber - *Chairperson, Communist Party of Austria, Tirol, Innsbruck, Austria*

H. Charfo - *Head of the Department of International Relations, Central Committee, Communist Party of Bohemia and Moravia, Prague*

Marina Drummer - *Community Futures Collective*

Brett de Bary - *Professor of Asian Studies, Cornell University*

Greg Ericson - *Founder, freepressinternational.com, Austin, Texas*

Justin Bendell - *Fuguers Cove Collective, Madison, Wisconsin*

Patrik Köbele - *Chairman, German Communist Party, Ruhr-Westfalen, Germany*

Giorgio Ellero - *Gruppo Zastava Trieste, Italy*

Dennis Apel - *Guadalupe Catholic Worker, Guadalupe, California*

Alex Plows - *Gwynedd and Mon Earth First!, Gwynedd, Wales*

Claudia Haydt - *board member, IMI-Informationsstelle Militarisierung, Tuebingen, Germany*

Tobias Pflueger - *chairman, IMI, Tuebingen, Germany*

Karim Lopez - *Institute for Mass Communications/ HYP-HOP, Brooklyn*

Hugh Stephens - *Secretary, Institute for Independence Studies, London, England*

Adam Blunt - International Action Center - *Bridgewater State College Chapter, Canton, Massachusetts*

Canadian-Cuban Friendship Association, Vancouver, Canada

Marília Rondani - *Núcleo de Meio Ambiente da União de Mulheres de São Paulo, Brasil*

Falco Accame - *former president of the Defense Commission in the Chamber of Deputies, Italian Tribunal on NATO crimes in Jugoslavia, Italy*

Peter Cadogan - *chairperson, London Alliance for Local Democracy, London, England*

Tim King - farmer, Long Prairie River Stewardship Project, Long Prairie, Minnesota

Media Monitors Network Southern (mediamonitors.net), California

Taijun Nishida - *No More War, Hiroshima, Japan*

Kevan Hudson - *Ogoni Solidarity Network, Richmond, British Columbia, Canada*

Joshua Thomason - *Oklahoma Socialist Cooperative, Chickasha, Missouri*

Joseph P. Horgan - *Shop steward - IBT shop, OPEIU Local 2, Kensington, Maryland*

Athos Fava - *Secretary for International Relations, Partido Comunista de la Argentina, Buenos Aires, Argentina*

Patricio Echegary - *General Secretary, Partido Comunista de la Argentina*

Elizabeth O'Nan - *Director, Protect All Children's Environment (PACE), Marion, North Carolina*

Judith Detert-Moriarty - *Rock County Citizens for Peace, Janesville, Wisconsin*

Wendy Strebe - *Rural Community Assistance, Las Vegas, Nevada*

David San Martín - *Sentimientos Kontra el Poder, Getafe (Madrid), Spain*

Bet Power - *Director, Sexual Minorities Archive, Northampton, Massachusetts*

Daniel Golovaty Cursino - *Shalom Salam Paz, Brasil*

Fausto Schiavetto - *Soccorso Popolare (Popular Aid) - Padova, Padova, Italy*

David A. Smith - *Editor, Social Problems, Irvine, California*

Spanish Campaign for Lifting the Sanctions on Iraq, Spain

Olivera Pavlovic - *doctor professor, Yugoslavia*

Aisha Sabadia - *Muslim Student Union, Amnesty, Ann Arbor, Michigan*

Susanne Kelly - *secretary-treasurer, Local 334 OPEIU, Richmond, Virginia*

Saif Bonar - *Surf London, London, England*

Thomas Claesson - *Teachers League of Sweden, Skärhamn, Tjörn, Sweden*

Justin Vitiello - *Professor of Italian, Temple University, Philadelphia*

Jamie York - *The Cuba Advocate Newsletter,
Deer Lodge, Montana*

Linda Wolf - *The Daughters Sisters Project,
Bainbridge Island, Washington*

Maher Kouraytem - *The Lebanese Communist Party,
Beirut, Lebanon*

United Public Housing Residents, Washington, DC

Judith Kegan Gardiner - *Professor of English and of Gender &
Women's Studies, University of Illinois at Chicago*

Claudio Moffa - *professor of History of Afro-Asian countries,
University of Teramo*

Vietnam Veterans Against The War Anti Imperialist

Voice of Yugo-Diaspora

Jutta Burghardt - *former Director, World Food Programme in
Iraq, Sankt Augustin, Netherlands*

Arthur Staats, PhD - *Professor (Emeritus) of Psychology*

Dale Sophiea and Elania Nanopoulos

Felicity Arbuthnot - *journalist, England*

Leila Sansour - *T.V. Producer, London, England*

Lester Schonbrun - *Oakland, California*

Muna Hamzeh - *author and journalist, Austin, Texas*

Riem Farahat - *Long Beach, California*

Seemin Qayum - *New York City*

Susan Peters - *New York City*

Keiko Kani - *researcher and environmental specialist, Konan,
Aichi, Japan*

Tracey McPartlan - *Director, 11th Hour Group, Lennox Head,
New South Wales, Australia*

N. Falciatano - *Animal Defense League, Los Angeles, California*

Donnie Quest - *student organizer, AxCx Punks,
Laramie, Wyoming*

Ross Stuart Marat - *Bedfordshire Socialist Alliance,
Luton, England*

Kathleen Semanski - *student activist, Boston University, West
Hartford, Connecticut*

Ian M. Betteridge - *Publishing Administrator, British Medical Journal, Brighton, East Sussex, England*

Phil Runkel - *archivist, Catholic Worker, Marquette University*

Hillel Barak - *Committee for One Democratic & Secular Republic, Beit Shemesh, Israel*

Kathryn M. Daly - *law student, CUNY Law School,*

Eduardo Unda Sanzana – *Dept. of Physics & Astronomy, University of Soton, Southampton, England*

Brian Shea - *Disabled Peoples Liberation Front, Boston*

Paul Davidson - *Euro-Cuba News, London, England*

Alexis Ponce - *Vocero Nacional, Asamblea Permanente de Derechos Humanos (APDH) del Ecuador, Quito*

Soledad Paz, Argentina

Bernd Hamm - *Jean Monnet Professor of European Studies, University of Trier, Germany*

Stratis Kounias - *University of Athens, Greece*

Grace de Haro - *APDH Human Rights Organization, Argentina*

Ramiro Gonzalez - *Argentina*

Martin S. Past - *coordinator of international activities, Peace Office Netherlands*

Wanda Colón Cortés - *Proyecto Caribeño de Justicia y Paz, San Juan, Puerto Rico*

Randolph Carter Richter - *First Church of Christ, Scientist, Denver & Boston, Lakewood, Colorado*

Dorothy Byrne - *Green Political Party, St. Petersburg, Florida*

Roz Rayner-Rix - *Hambleton Area Belly Dance Association, Dalton, Thirsk, England*

Mickey Gibson - *Harmonic Arts/West, Bainbridge Island, Washington*

Michael Gene Ratkewicz - *Account Executive, HotJobs.com, San Francisco*

Tomiyama Ichiro - *staff member, IMPACTION, Kyoto, Japan*

Mindy Stone - *Indian River Green Party, Vero Beach, Florida*

William D. Fusfield - *Associate Professor, University of Pittsburgh*

Tony Robertson - *Community Worker, Micah, Inc., South Brisbane, Australia*

Nick Valvo - *student, Oberlin College*

Eric Scheinert - *Ryan White Care Council, PHHASE, Inc. Compassion House, Lakeland, Florida*

Joan Clingan - *educator and anti-racist, Prescott College Master of Arts Program, Prescott, Arizona*

Brent Buell - *writer, Professional Staff Congress, New York City*

Bobbie Dee Flowers - *College Assistant/Site Coordinator, RB/LIU, New York City*

Steven Schroeder - *Instructor in Philosophy, Roosevelt University, Chicago*

Tian Harter - *Santa Clara County Green Party, Mountain View, California*

Mick Dunford - *School of European Studies, University of Sussex, Brighton, England*

David Muller - *South Movement, Melbourne, Victoria, Australia*

Dave Havard - *Deacon, St. Margaret's Anglican Church, Vancouver, Canada*

Nancy Bauer - *Assistant Professor of Philosophy, Tufts University*

Nathan A. Hawks - *webmaster, WarOnWar.org, Metairie, Louisiana*

Kristin Andrews - *Facilitator, Watauga Green Party, Banner Elk, North Carolina*

Stephanie Carlisle - *Wesleyan University, Middletown, Connecticut*

Damien Lawson - *Western Suburbs Legal Service, Newport, Victoria, Australia*

Norwood Orrick - *Programmer, WMNF Community Radio, Tampa, Florida*

Dhruti Contractor - *Graduate Student, Yale University*

Michael Petrs - *Young Democratic Socialists, Avon Lake, Ohio*

rev les ego - *Linguistics Editor, Zentences, New York City*

David Klein - *in-home-services social worker, SEIU, Altadena, California*

Alex Holcombe - *organizer, San Diego Coalition for Peace and Justice.*

Diane McKay - *adjunct professor, Rutgers University, New York City*

Stefano Perale - *dottore, Manitese-Venezia, Ve-Mestre, Italy*

Sheila Howlett - *Peace Activist, Kawartha Ploughshares, Peterborough, Ontario*

Kristen Gregg - *marketing director, HEAL Foundation, Memphis, Tennessee*

Teddy Yoshikami - *public and multicultural programming, American Museum of Natural History, Brooklyn*

Audrey Williams - *President Afrimerica, Inc., The African Stock Exchange Development Corporation, Dover, Delaware*

Mary Zoeter - *ESL tutor and president, Action for Animals Network, Alexandria, Virginia*

Victoria D. Gaines - *psychiatric escapee and activist, Hagertown, Maryland*

Dianne S. Lobes - *peace activist, WAND, Eugene, Oregon*

Robert Lophovsky - *adjunct faculty, University of Dayton, Ohio*

Allen Campbell - *Edgemere, New York*

Cary Birdsall - *teacher, Talkeetna, Alaska*

Chris "The Anarchist" Ryan - *community organizer and activist, Columbus, Ohio*

Emily Roscia - *recent law graduate*

Margot Sheehan - *writer and graphic artist, Hoboken, New Jersey*

Maribeth Botts - *writer and musician, LaFeria, Texas*

Noriko Kokubun - *university professor, Yokohama, Japan*

Oona Besman - *academic and activist, Columbus, Ohio*

Randy Richter - *service administrator, Lakewood, Colorado*

2. Not In Our Name (Partial Endorsements) and NION Pledge

Organizations include:

Action Center For Justice * African American Institute for Policy Studies and Planning * African American Lawyers Association-Hawaii * AltBuzz * Alternative Tenticles * American Arab Anti Discrimination Committee * American Muslim Voice * Bay Area United Against War * Blue Triangle Network * Chelsea for Peace * Clergy of the Soko Bukai * Code Pink * Engineers and Scientists for Animal Rights * Freedom Socialist Party * Georgia Peace and Justice Coalition, Atlanta * Hawai`i Labor for Peace and Justice * Idriss Stelley Foundation * Interfaith Freedom Foundation * La Raza Centro Legal * National 911Visibility.org Movement * Network in Solidarity with the People of the Philippines * New York City Labor Against the War * Not in Our Name * `Ohana Koa / Nuclear Free and Independent Pacific * Puerto Rican Alliance of Los Angeles * Refuse and Resist! * SF Day Laborers * South Asians Against Police Brutality and Racism * South Bay Mobilization, San Jose * South Philadelphias Together Against Bush * The Foundry Theatre * The Lorax Society * The Northeast Ohio Anti-War Coalition * Ukuleles for Sanity * University of Hawai`i Peace Initiative * Vietnam Veterans Against the War Anti-Imperialist * Women's International League for Peace & Freedom, NY Metro Chapter

Individuals include:

Ashton Applewhite (writer) * Edward Asner (actor) * Eleanor J Bader * Anne Balay * Russell Banks * Fay S Barrows * Kristina Bell * Medea Benjamin * Jello Biafra (artist) * William G Bird Jr * Jessica Blank (actor and playwright) * Marcia Bollea * Dr T Bowers * Barbara Braunstein * Sheila Levrant de Bretteville (professor) * Julia Butterfly (environmental activist) * John Cassella * Rev Robert W Castle * Henry Chalfant (photographer and filmmaker) * Kathleen Chalfant (actor) * Nancy Chang (attorney) * Vanessa Chong (Exec Dir of ACLU-Hawai`i) * Reed Christian * Thomas A Copeland * Peter Coyote (actor) * Charles Craig * Michael Curi * Chris Daly (SF City Supervisor) * Kevin Danaher * Ed Desmond (Navy Vietnam era veteran) * Dick

Dettrey * Mark Diorio * Ross Duncan * Eve Ensler * Riva
Enteen * Julia Estrella * Larry Evans * Larry Everest (author)
* Elena Featherston * Nina Felshin (curator) * Fishbone
(musicians) * Sally Fisher * Shem Fleenor * Geri Fox * Reg E
Gaines (poet) * Danny Glover (actor) * John J Glynn * Frances
Goldin (literary agent) * Leon Golub (artist) * Michael Gray *
Kathryn Greene * Cheryl Guerbaoui * Anna Hall * Wes
Hamilton * Joy Harjo (poet) * P Thomas Harker * Nancy CM
Hartsock * Brock Hastie * Robert I Hattem * Grace M Hawkins
* Tom Hayden * Jen Hazlett * James Adam Holland III * Mesha
Monge Irizarry * Ron Jacobs * David Jaeger * Clarice Jensen *
Earl Johnson * Ricki Lee Jones (musician) * Melanie Joseph *
Kyle Kajihiro (Exec Dir of AFSC-Hawai`i) * Casey Kasem (radio
personality) * Jean Khatchadourian * C Clark Kissinger
(contributing writer, Revolutionary Worker) * Yuri Kochiyama *
Rev Dr Earl Kooperkamp * Joyce Kozloff (artist) * Tom
Krebsbach * Rev Peter Laarman (Exec Dir of Progressive
Christians Uniting, LA) * Pierre Labossiere * Beth K Lamont *
Greg Landau (music producer) * Jesse Lemisch * Giovanna
Lepore * Brett Lewis * Barbara Lubin (Middle East Children's
Alliance) * Eric Mar (SF Board of Education) * Gayle Marra *
William Martinez * Patricia Mason * Carollen Mathieu * Sean
McCollough * A Q McElrath * Ralph McKnight * Pat
McManaman (immigrant rights attorney) * Cody Mitchell *
Miguel Gavilan Molina (KPFA radio) * Robert Alex Monroe, Jr
* Katalina Montero * Cynthia Monsour * Jude Rene Montarsi *
Angelo Moore (musician) * Patty Morlan * Roberta J Morgan *
Nettie Morano * Maya Morris * Susan Mosca * Clifford R
Moseley * Joseph J Mueller * Johnathan C Mulhall * Jessica
Murillo * Kevin O'Neill * Jill Nelson (author and activist) * Osha
Newman (civil rights attorney) * Rev-Dr Penny Nixon
(Metropolitan Community Church of SF) * Kate Noonan *
Roxanne Dunbar Ortiz (professor) * Michael Parenti * Geraldine
M Parker * Eva Patterson (Equal Justice Society, SF) * Hon Bill
Perkins (NY City Council) * Rosalind Petchesky * Jeremy Pikser
(screenwriter-Bulworth) * Assad Pino * Frances Fox Piven
(CUNY Faculty Grad Center) * Peter Preszon * Margaret
Randall (writer and photographer) * Rev George F Regas
(Interfaith Communities United For Justice and Peace) * Reno

158

(actor) * Adrienne Rich (poet and writer) * Wilson Riles * Syed Rizvi (Engineers and Scientists for Animal Rights) * Robie Robledo * Robert Rockwell (National Secretary of Refuse & Resist!) * David Rubinson * Jennifer Martin Ruggiero * Mustafa Sallak * Sonia Sanchez (poet) * James Schamus (professor) * Edmund A Schofield, Jr * Derek Shevel * Laurie Sheridan * Savannah Skye * Nicolai Sokulski * Nancy Spero (artist) * Art Spiegelman (cartoonist) * Bob Stein (The Voyager Company) * Mary Stiel * Michael Stoegbauer * Brian K Sullwold * Esther Surovell * Linda Sue Swisher * Christopher Szell * Kathryn W B Takara (poet) * Silvia Tennenbaum * Kortni Tracy * Dean Tuckerman * Julienne Verdi * Richard Washbourne * Thomas Webster * Len Weinglass (attorney) * Naomi Weisstein * Robert West * Saul Williams (artist) * Dan Wilson * Bob Wing (editor, War Times) * Billy Wolfsthal * Ali Yahiaoui * Douglass Young * Sue Zimmerman * Howard Zinn (writer and historian) * Paul H Zulkowitz

NION Pledge of Resistance

We believe that as people living
in the United States it is our
responsibility to resist the injustices
done by our government,
in our names
Not in our name
will you wage endless war
there can be no more deaths
no more transfusions
of blood for oil
Not in our name
will you invade countries
bomb civilians, kill more children
letting history take its course
over the graves of the nameless
Not in our name
will you erode the very freedoms
you have claimed to fight for
Not by our hands
will we supply weapons and funding

for the annihilation of families
on foreign soil
Not by our mouths
will we let fear silence us
Not by our hearts
will we allow whole peoples
or countries to be deemed evil
Not by our will
and Not in our name
We pledge resistance
We pledge alliance with those
who have come under attack
for voicing opposition to the war
or for their religion or ethnicity
We pledge to make common cause
with the people of the world
to bring about justice,
freedom and peace
Another world is possible
and we pledge to make it real.

3. UNITED FOR PEACE AND JUSTICE
Member Groups (partial list):

1199'ers for Peace and Justice
20/20 Vision
5th Congressional District Neighbors for Peace
9/11 Coalition
A World of Women for World Peace
A.W.O.L.
Aaron Patterson Defense Committee
Abolition 2000 New York
Academics For Justice
Action Center for Justice
Activist San Diego
African Youth Movement on the Environment, Nigeria
African-American Women's Clergy Association
Afrikan-American Institute for Policy Studies
Afrique Development, Cote D'Ivoire

AFSCME Local 2858
AidLit
Al-Awda, Palestine Right to Return Coalition - CT Chapter
All Pakistan Federation of United Trade Unions (APFTU)
All Souls Church, Unitarian Universalist
Alliance for Democracy Capital Dist NY
American Arab Anti-Discrimination Committee (ADC)
American Friends Service Committee – Hawai'i Area Program,
    Vermont, Africa Initiative, Chicago, Int. Program
    Executive Com, Iowa Program, National Youth &
    Military, New England Regional, Pacific Southwest
    Region, Washingtion D.C.
American Muslims for Jerusalem
American Renaissance
Americans Against War in Prague/International Peace
Americans for Social Justice
An Absurd Response to an Absurd War
Ann Arbor Coalition Against the War
Ann Arbor Mobilization for Global Justice
Anti-Capitalist Convergence
Anti-Imperialist News Service
AntiWar Video Fund
Antiwar.com
AntiwarStudents.com
April6Vt Lobby
Arab Student Union, University of Michigan-Dearborn
Architects/Designers/Planners for Social Responsibility
Arizona Alliance for Peaceful Justice
Arizona Green Party
Arkansas Coalition for Peace and Justice
Arlington United for Justice with Peace
Artist Action Network
ASD
Asian American Movement E-zine
Astorians For Peace and Justice
Attorneys Against the War
Aurora We The People Peace & Justice Coalition
AWARE (Anti-War Anti-Racism Effort)
Aware Movement

Bay Area Pax Christi
Bay Area United Against War
Ben&Jerry's/TrueMajority/Business Leaders
Bethlehem Neighbors for Peace- C.A.P.
Wood River Peace Coalition
Black Radical Congress
Black Solidarity Against War at Home and Abroad
Black Voices for Peace
Black Workers for Justice
Bobotees.com
Boston College Global Justice Project
Boston Mobilization
Boston United for Justice with Peace
BostontoPalestine, Friends of Haley House, Boston
Brandywine Peace Community
Brattleboro Peace and Justice Group
Brecht Forum
Brockport Students Against War (BSAW)
Brookdale Community Action: a SPAN affiliate
Brookline PeaceWorks
Brooklyn Demilitarized Zone project (BkDMZ)
Brooklyn Heights Peace Action
Brooklyn Parents for Peace
Brooklyn Society for Ethical Culture
Brooklyn Society for Ethical Culture, Peace Site
Broward Anti War Coalition
Broward Bill of Rights Defense Coalition
Buddhist Peace Fellowship
Buddhist Peace Fellowship - Pioneer Valley Chapter
Buffalo State Students for Peace
Bustan Al Salaam for Development & Relief Association
California Peace Action
Cambridge UJP
Camp Kinderland
Campaign for Peace and Democracy
Campaign on Contingent Work
Campus Greens
Cape Codders for Peace and Justice
Carlessnesshood 101 for Healthier Air, Planet & People

Catholic Worker
Center for Community Change
Center for Constitutional Rights
Center for Economic and Social Research
Center for Human Rights Transformation
Center for Immigrant Families (CIF)
Center for International Policy
Center for Religion, Ethics, and Social Policy at Cornell University
Center for Social Justice
Center on Race, Poverty & the Environment
Central American Resource Center (CARECEN)
Central Florida Jobs Committee
Central Indiana Alliance for Peace and Justice
Central Iowa Students for Peace
Central Kentucky Witness of Conscience
Central Nebraska Peace Workers
Centre for Social Justice / CSJ Foundation for Res
Change the Game
Charleston Peace
Charlotte Coalition for Peace & Justice
Chicago ADAPT
Chicago Caravan Committee
Chicago Committee to Free Mumia Abu-Jamal
Chicago Cuba Committee
Chicago Jobs With Justice
Chicago Labor Against the War
Chicago Labor for Peace and Justice
Chicago Media Action
Chicago Media Watch
Chicagoans Against War in Iraq
Church Women United
CIT & Educational Consultancy, Nepal
Citizen Works
Citizens for Legitimate Government
Citizens for Participation in Political Action (CPPAX)
Citizens for Peace
Citizens for Peace & Justice
CitizenSpeak
City College Coalition for Peace and Justice

City Council District 7 Housing Taskforce
Cleveland Noviolence Network (CNVN)
Coalition Against Global Exploitation (CAGE)
Coalition Against the War on Civil Liberties
Coalition for Civil Liberties
Coalition for Civil Liberties
Coalition for Peace Action
Coalition for Peace and Justice, Linwood, NJ
Coalition for Radical Enlightenment (C.O.R.E.)
Coalition for World Peace
Coalition of Labor Union Women-Chicago
Coalition to End the Cycle of Violence
Code Pink
CodePink4Peace
Coffeehouse Teach-ins
Coles County for Peace and Justice
Coles for Peace
Collectif Echec a la guerre
Collier County Anti-war Coalition
Colorado Campaign for Mid East Peace
Colorado Coalition Against the War on Iraq
Columbia Antiwar Coalition, NY/NJ Campus Antiwar
Columbus Campaign for Arms Control
Committee for Human Rights in the Philippines
Committee for New Priorities
Committee for Peace and Social Justice, Nigeria
Committee on Women, Population and the Environment (CWPE)
Committee to Free Pedro Pacheco
Committees of Correspondence for Democracy and
        Socialism (CCDS)
Communist Party - Maryland
Communist Party - New York
Communist Party- Central Indiana
Communist Party USA
Community of Faith for Peace of Williamsburg
Concerned Families of Westchester
Concerned Students and Faculty of St. Augustine Prep
Cooper Response Committee
Corporate Lawyers Against War

Council of Churches of the City of New York
Council on Civic Affairs
Counterconvention.org
Crocus Hill Neighbors for Peace and Justice
Culture of Peace News Network
DAWN, DuPage Against War Now
DC Alliance for Democracy
DC Anti-War Network (DAWN)
DC Poets Against the War
DC Statehood Green Party
DeKalb Interfaith Network for Peace and Justice
Delaware County Wage Peace & Justice
Democractic Socialism Club of Bethel College
Democracy In Action
Democracy North Carolina
Democracy Rising
Democratic Alliance
Democratic Socialists of America
Democratic Socialists of America, Chicago chapt
Detroit Area Peace With Justice Network
Disarm Education Fund
DRC, Indonesia
DressKing Inc.
Dubuque Peace and Justice
DuPage Campus Greens
DuPage County Green Party
DuPage Peace Through Justice Coalition
Dutchess County Peace Coalition
Earth Rights Institute
East End Women in Black
East Enders United for Peace and Justice
Ecological Options Network (EON)
Education for Peace in Iraq Center (EPIC)
Educators for Social Responsibililty, Metro Area
El Dorado Peace & Justice Community
El Puente Coalition for Peace and Justice
Ella Baker Center for Human Rights
Emergency Committee To Defend Constitutional
        Welfare Rights, USA

Episcopal Peace Fellowship
Episcopal Peace Fellowship of Alabama
equality.justice.peace.organisation
Esteria Woods international outreach foundation
Evanston Mennonite Peace & Social Concerns Committee
Faculty for Peace and Justice-CSU
Fair Elections
Fairbanks Coalition for Peace and Justice
Families for Freedom
FAST/AFL-CIO
Fayetteville Peace with Justice
Fellowship of Reconciliation
Fellowship Of Reconciliation - Charlotte, NC
Fellowship of Reconciliation – Chicago
Feminist Peace Network
Fever Pitch Magazine & Music
Food not Bombs
Food Not Bombs - Muncie, IN
Food Not Bombs - New Haven, CT
Food Not Bombs - San Francisco and East Bay, CA
FootPrints for Peace
Foreign Policy in Focus
Fort Myers Social Action Committee
Fort Wayne Peace Action Coalition
Forum for Human Rights
Four Lakes Green Party
Fourth Freedom Foundation
Fox Peace Coalition
Fox Valley Peace Coalition
Framingham Ethical Action League
FREE CUNY
Freedom Road Socialist Organization
Friends of the Earth
Frontlines Newspaper
General Board of Global Ministries United Methodist Church
Georgetown Peace Action
Georgetown University Law Center Chapter
Georgia Peace Coalition
Global Exchange

Global Network Against Weapons & Nuclear Power in Space
Global Peace Action
Global Resource Action Center for the Environment (GRACE)
Got Peace?
Goucher Peace and Justice League
Government Affairs Consultant
Grandmothers for Peace International
Grandmothers for Peace, Cape Cod Chapter
Grandmothers for Peace, Las Vegas
Grassroots International
Greater Bangor Area Veterans for Peace, Chapter 003
Greater Milwaukee Green Party
Greater New Haven Peace Council
Greater New York Labor-Religion Coalition
Greater Warren Against the War
Green Alliance
Green Dove
Green House of Metro Detroit
Green Mountain Peace
Green Party - Florida, Pinellas County; Lancaster, PA;
        New Jersey; New York; Ohio; Tennessee; Texas,
        Harris County; United States; Utah Greenpeace
Ground Zero for Peace - 9/11 First Responders Against War
GTM
Guerrero Azteca Project
H.E.R.E. Local 1
Hadley Green-Rainbow Party
Hague Appeal For Peace
Harlem Anti-war Coalition
HealthWrights
Heartwood
Helena Peace Seekers
Hip-Hop Against Racist War
Historians Against the War
Horizons Community Services
Hotel Employees and Restaurant Employees Union, Local 1
House of The Goddess Center for Pagan Wombyn
House of the Lord Church
Hudson County Coalition for Peace and Justice

Human Rights Activists for Peace
Humanist Center of Cultures
Huntington Woods Peace, Citizen Education Project
Hyde Parkers against War in Iraq
Idaho Green Party
Idaho Peace Coalition
Iliff School of Theology, Social Action Committee
Illinois Peace Action
Illinois Socialist Party
In These Times
Independent Progressive Politics Network
Indiana Green Party
Inlandpeace Coalition
Instead of War
Instead of War- St. Louis
Institute for Policy Studies
Institute for Public Accuracy
Institute of Southern Studies
Intercommunity Justice and Peace Center (IJPC)
InterFaith Committee on Latin America
Interfaith Communities United for Justice and Peace
International Socialist Organization
International Solidarity Movement (ISM), North America
Iowa Peace Network
Iranian Women for Peace
Iraq Pledge of Resistance
ISAR
Jamaica Plain Action Network
Jewish Voice for Peace
Jews Against The Occupation (JAtO)
Jews for Peace in Palestine and Israel (JPPI)
Jews for Racial & Economic Justice
John Denver Peace Cloth
June 1st Peace Coalition
Justice and Peace Ministry, First Congregational Church,
        United Church of Christ
Justice For Detainees
Justice for Woody
Justice Studies Association

Justice with Peace Task Force of Watertown Citizens for
    Environmental Safety
Kalamazoo Non-violent Opponents of War (KNOW)
Kansas City Labor Against War
Kensington Welfare Rights Union
KhaYUMbia
Knights of the Socially Conscious
Konscious Media
Korean-American Resource & Cultural Center
Labone Branch of Ghana United Nations Association
Lafayette Area Peace Coalition
Lafayette Committee for Israeli/Palestinian Peace and Justice
Lakes Region Peace and Justice Group
Lamar University Southeast Texans Organized for Peace
Lambertville Coalition for Peace (LCFP)
Lamorinda Peace and Justice Group
Lancaster Peace Coalition
LaSalle Co. Citizens for Peace
Latinos & Latinas for Peace and Justice
Latinos Por La Paz
Latinos Unidos por la Justicia - Lawrence, MA
Lavender Block
Lawyers' Committee on Nuclear Policy
League of Revolutionaries for a New America
League of Young Voters
Left Party
Left Turn
Lehigh Valley Peace Coalition
Lehigh-Pocono Committee of Concern (LEPOCO)
let there be light peace foundation
Lexington Justice and Peace Committee
Liberation Alliance for Change (LAC), Nigeria
Lincoln Park Neighbors United For Peace, Chicago
Logan Square Neighbors for Justice and Peace
LOKOJ, Bangladesh
Long Beach Area Peace Network (LBAPN)
Long Island Alliance for Peaceful Alternatives
Longfellow Neighbors for Peace
Lusory

M27 Coalition
Madison Area Peace Coalition & National Network to MADRE,
    An International Women's Human Rights Organization
Maine Coalition for Peace and Justice
Maine Vets For Peace
Malibu Citizens for Peace
Manchester Area People for Peace
Manhattan Alliance for Peace and Justice
MARHO: The Radical Historians Organization
Martha's Vineyard Peace Council
Maryknoll Mission Association of the Faithful
Maryknoll Office for Global Concerns
Maui Peace Action
McHenry County Peace Group
MECAWI – Gray Panthers of MI
Mennonite Central Committee UN Office
Merriam Park Neighbors for Peace
Merrimack Valley People For Peace
Metro DC Committee of Correspondence
Metro. Chgo. General Mtg. of Friends
Mexico Solidarity Network
Michigan Coalition for Human Rights
Middle East Children's Alliance
Middle East Crisis Committee, New Haven
Middle East Research and Information Project (MERIP)
Midland Citizens for Peace
Mighty Companions
Military Families Speak Out (MFSO)
Milwaukee Pledge of Resistance
Minneapolis/5th District Green Party
Missing Kitten TV
Mobilize New York
Monroe for Peace and Justice
Morris Area Peace Seekers
Mothers Acting Up
Movement for Democratic Socialism (MDS)
MoveOn
Mt. Diablo Peace Center
Music Therapists for Peace, Inc.

N.E.W. Peace Network, Northeast Wisconsin
Nashville Peace and Justice Center
National Alliance Against Racist and Political Repression
National Coalition for Peace and Justice
National Council of Churches
National Day Laborer Organizing Network
National Lawyers Guild
National Lawyers Guild - Milw. Chapter
National Lawyers Guild, NYC Chapter
National Network on Cuba
National Network to End the War Against Iraq
National Organization for Women (NOW)
National Organization of People Against War Now
National Organizers Alliance
National Student Front University of Indonesia, Indonesia
National War Tax Resistance Coordinating Committee
National Writers Union, Philadelphia District 8
National Youth Advocacy Coalition
National Youth and Student Peace Coalition
NC Peace Action
Nebraskans for Peace
Neighbors for Peace
Neighbors United for Justice and Peace
Network in Solidarity with the People of the Philippines (NISPOP)
NETWORK, A National Catholic Social Justice Lobby
New Jersey Civil Rights Defense Committee
New Justice System
New School Students Against War
New York City Baptist Peace Ministries
New York City Labor Against the War (NYCLAW)
New York Coalition for Peace & Justice, Brecht Forum
New York Youth Bloc
New Yorkers Say No to War
NH Peace Action
Nigerian Youth Against Conflict, Nigeria
NJ Peace Action
No Blood For Oil
Nodutdol for korean community development
Nonviolent Peaceforce

North Coast Peace Coalition
North Essex Community College Coalition for Peace
North Manhattan Neighbors for Peace and Justice
North West Ohio Peace Coalition
Northbranch Green Party
Northeast Ohio Antiwar Coalition
Northern Coalition for Peace and Justice
Northern Manhattan Neighbors for Peace and Justice
Northern Utah Peace Alliance
Northern Virginians for Peace
Northwest Central Labor Council AFL-CIO
Not In My Name
Not In Our Name
Not In Our Name (NION) - Chicago Chapter
Not In Our Name (NION) - Houston
Not In Our Name (NION) - Santa Barbara
Not In Our Name (NION)- NYC
Not In Our Name Youth and Student Network
Now End War and Sanctions on Iraq
Nowar Collective
Nuclear Age Peace Foundation
Nukewatch
NYC Forum of Concerned Religious Leaders
NYU Inc
NYU Peace Coalition
Oak Park Coalition for Truth and Justice
Oberlin Students for a Free Palestine
Occidental Anti-War Coalition
Office of the Americas
OneWorld Peace Foundation
Orange County Peace& Justice Coalition
Oregon Peace Works
Outer Cape Peace and Justice Circle
Ozark Heritage Region Peace Network
Pacifica Foundation
Pacifica Peace People
Pakistan Democratic Peace Party
Pakistan FATA Peace Forum, Pakistan
Pakistan International Peace & Human Rights Organization

Parents Coalition to End High Stakes Testing
Parents for Peace
Partido Socialista del Valle - SP USA Local
Partners for Peace
Pax Christi Michigan
Pax Christi Naples
Pax Christi Springfield
Pax Christi USA
Peace & Justice Committee - St. Francis Xavier Church
Peace & Justice Petitioners
Peace & Social Justice Center of South Central Kansas
Peace 2000 Institute
Peace Action - Kapiti, New Zealand; Michigan; New Hampshire;
        New Jersey; New Mexico; New York State;
        North Carolina; Staten Island; Wisconsin
Peace and Hope
Peace and Justice Center of Sonoma County
Peace and Justice Committee of Capital District Greens
Peace and Justice Task Force, Rocky Mountain Conference,
        United Church of Christ
Peace and Justice Works
Peace and Social Justice Center
Peace and Social Justice Center of South Central Kansas
Peace Asia
Peace Aware
Peace Café
Peace Economy Project
Peace Foundation International PFI, Nigeria
Peace Group of Africa Students, Nigeria
Peace House
Peace In the Middle East
Peace Initiative Turkey
Peace Resource Center of San Diego
Peace South Florida
Peace Train Coalition
Peace Vigilers - PeaceVigils.com
PeaceAndJustice
PeaceAware
PeaceAware.com

Peaceful Justice
PeaceMongers Society
PeaceNoWar
PeaceRoots Alliance
PeaceWilliamsburg
PeaceWorks
Peninsula Peace and Justice Center
Pennsylvania Lesbian and Gay Task Force
People Against Oppression and War
People for a Gasoline-Free Day
People for Peace and Justice
People for Peace and Justice of Utah (PPJ)
People for Peace and Justice, York, PA
People for Peace, Justice, and Healing
People of Color United for Justice and Peace
People of Color United for Justice and Peace, Baltimore Chapter
People's Global Action Network
Peoples NonViolent Response Coalition (PNVRC)
People's Organization for Progress
Peoria Area Peace Network
Pertubuhan Gerak Seni Silat Abjad (Asli) Jabat Kilat
    Malaysia Kelantan
Petalumans Against War
Philadelphia Solidarity
Pittsburgh Palestine Solidarity Committee
Planning For Peace
Pledge of Resistance/Baltimore
PLURtopia & Enlightened Libra Creations
Plymouth Congregational United Church of Christ
Pocatello For Peace
Polaris Institute
Port Townsend Peace Movement
Portland Peaceful Response Coalition
Pride At Work, AFL-CIO
Professionals' Network for Social Responsibility
Progress OWU (Ohio Wesleyan University)
Progressive Business Network
Progressive Peace Coalition
Project Kesher

Promoting Enduring Peace
Psychoanalysts for Peace and Justice
Psychologists for Social Responsibility
Psychotherapists and Mental Health Workers for
    Social Responsibility
Queer to the Left
Queers for Economic Justice
Queers For Peace and Justice
Queers For Racial & Economic Justice
Quixote Center
Racine Coalition for Peace and Justice
Raelian Religion
Raging Grannies
Raging Grannies - Peninsula, CA
Rainbow/Push Coalition
Rainforest Action Network
RallyofOne.org
RANT - Root Activist Network of Trainers
RANT - Root Activist Network of Trainers, Pagan cluster
Refuse+Resist, Not In Our Name
Reno Anti-War Coalition
Resources Unlimited Foundation
Restaurant Opportunities Center of New York
Rhode Islanders for Peace
Rice For Peace
Riconciliazione.it, Italy
Rockefeller University for Peace
Rooting Out Evil
Rosary Foundation
Act Right Nigeria
Women in Black, Knoxville Area Chapter
Beyond Today
Rouge Forum
RPCAN
RU for Peace
Ruckus Society
Rural Organizing Project
Rural Peacemakers
San Diego Coalition for Peace and Justice

San Juan County Peace Coalition
San Mateo County League of United Latin American Citizens
    (LULAC)
San Miguel Peacewalkers
San Pedro Neighbors for Peace and Justice
Satyagraha
School of the Americas Watch (SOAW)
Seattle Peace Chorus
Secure Future
Seeds of Peace
Seniors Organized for Justice
September 11th Families for Peaceful Tomorrows
Shalom Center
Shepherd College Green Party
Shobak.Org (Outsider Asian Voices)
Sierra Interfaith Action For Peace
Silverton People for Peace
Sisters of Notre Dame de Namur
SNOW (Sound Nonviolent Opponents to War)
SOA Watch
Social Action Committe, Third Unitarian Church
Social Action Connection
Social Justice Committee, Universalist Unitarian Fellowship,
    DeKalb
Socialist Action
Socialist Alternative
Socialist Organization for Relief, Tradition, and Opposing Fascism
Socialist Party USA
Socialist Party, Ohio chapter
Sojourners
Solidarity; Detroit Branch and Madison Branch
South Florida Peace and Justice Network
South Valley Peace Center
Southeast Missouri Coalition For Peace and Justice
Southern Peace Research and Education Center
Speak Out Against War in Iraq
Speak Truth to Power Tour: Generation Hip Hop Says No to War
Speakers for a New America
Spirit House

Springs Action Alliance/ Pikes Peak Justice and Peace
St. Francis Xavier Peace & Justice Committee
St. Louis Area Anti-War Activism Committee
St. Louis Instead of War Coalition
St. Luke's Evangelical Fellowship
St.Paul's Forward Educational Society, Pakistan
Stand Up New York
Stark County Peace Coalition
Stop On Sunday
Stop the War Action Mask Project, Korea
Stop War On Iraq
Strategic Pastoral Action
Student Environmental Action Coalition (SEAC)
Student Peace Action Network (SPAN)
Student Peace Action Network, Syracuse Chapter
Student Solidarity Network -NYC
Students Against Sanctions and War in Iraq
Students Against Social Injustice (SASI), McKendree College
Students Against Testing
Students Against War - UTK
Students for Peace and Justice at MSU, Michigan
Students for Peace in Iraq Now, Wesleyan University
Students Take Action for New Directions (STAND)
Students Transforming and Resisting Corporations (STARC)
Students United for a Responsible Global Environment
Sullivan Peace and Justice
SUSTAIN (Stop US Tax-funded Aid to Israel Now)
SUSTAIN - New Hampshire
SW Colorado Peace & Justice Coalition
Synthesis - Wallkill High School
Syracuse Cultural Workers
Syracuse Peace Council
T:AP Refugees Project , Norway
Takhleeq Foundation
Taking Aim
Tallahassee Network for Justice and Peace
Terre Haute Stop War on Iraq
Texans for Peace
Thau Relief Agency

The Advanced Institute
The Arab-American Forum
The Connected Collective
The Global Plan Initiative
The North Coast Peace Coalition
The Peace Farm
The Roots International
The Tenants' and Workers' Support Committee / Comite de
    Apoyo de Inquilinos y Trabajadores
The Thomas Paine Project
The United Students of São Paulo, Brazil
The Voice Of The World
Theaters Against War (THAW)
ThinkingPeople
Thomas Merton Center - Pittsburgh
ThomasMc.com
Tikkun Community
Tikkun, Santa Fe
TokyoProgressive
Topanga Peace Alliance
TransAfrica Forum
Traprock Peace Center
Tri-City Action for Peace
Tri-Valley Communities Against and Radioactive Environment
    (CAREs)
TrueMajority
Two-Edged Sword Incorporated
U.S. Student Association
UE District 2
UMCP Peace Forum
Umm Al-Qura International, Pakistan
Undisputed Truth
Unitarian Universalist Service Committee
Unite for Peace
United for Justice With Peace - Cambridge
United for Justice With Peace - Domerville/Medford
United for Justice With Peace - Jamaica Plain
United for Peace - Pierce County
United for Peace - Thurston County

United for Peace & Justice - Bay Area
United for Peace & Justice - NYC
United NY Black Radical Congress
United People 4 Peace
United States Student Association
United Students Against Sweatshops (USAS)
Unity
Universal Living Wage
University of Baltimore Progressives
University of Maryland, College Park Peace Forum (UMCP
       Peace Forum)
University of Pennsylvania Penn-For-Peace
Upper Valley Peace & Justice Group
Uptown for Peace & Justice
Uptown Multi Cultural Art
Urban Academy
UrgentCall.org
US Campaign to End the Israeli Occupation
US Peace Council
US Peace Council - MI Chapter
UT Watch
Vancouver for Peace
Vanguard Public Foundation
Venice Peace Coalition
Veterans for Common Sense
Veterans For Peace
Veterans for Peace - Chapter 0231
Veterans For Peace - Chapter 50, Michigan
Veterans for Peace - Maine
Vieques Support Campaign
Vietnam Veterans Against the War
Voices in the Wilderness
Voter March, Ltd.
Vukani Mawethu
WAND
War Resisters League - Executive Committee and
      Disarmament Group; Texas; West
War Times
Wasatch Coalition for Peace and Justice
Washington Peace Center

Watertown Citizens for Environmental Safety/Justice
Wesleyan Students for Peace in Iraq Now
WESPAC Foundation
West Sonoma County Women's Peace Group
Western NC Peace Coalition
Western New York Peace Center
Western States Legal Foundation
Wheels of Justice
WI Network for Peace and Justice
Win Without War
Winnebago (WI) Peace & Justice Center
Witness for Peace Great Lakes
Women Against War
Women Against War, Parents Coalition
Women for Justice and Peace in Iran
Women in Black
Women in Black, Gulfcoast, Florida
Women in Black, NYC
Women's Action for New Directions (WAND)
Women's International League For Peace and Freedom (WILPF)
Workers Party
Working Assets
World Citizens for Peace
World Federalist Association
World Federalist Association, Milwaukee, WI
World Homoeopathic Research & Education Organization
World Trade Center Witnesses United for Peace
Worldwide Renaissance
York County Greens, South Carolina
Young Communist League, USA
Young Democratic Socialists
Young Koreans United of Chicago
Young Koreans United of USA
Young Peoples Socialist League
Youth Crime Watch of the Gambia
Youth for Peace in Wisconsin
Youth for Peace, Wisconsin
Youth for Socialist Action
Z Magazine and ZNET

Compared to the voluminous literature on America's military past, the literature on the anti-war movement is, for reasons that are perhaps obvious, marginal to most history. There is little glory in opposition, and the legacy of dissent cannot compare with the profound role of warfare and conflict in shaping the destiny of men and nations. Having acknowledged that reality, it is equally important to note that the public record of dissent from war has a unique place in American history, including both the successes of the movement and—even more pointedly—its systemic and repeated failures.

War continues to dominate government and society, and it overwhelms the best energies of peace movements. Our huge military budgets and the dedication of whole segments of society to defense activities, plus the allure of modern technology, attest both to the continuing domination of a strategic military "culture" and the enduring failure of peace movements to affect politics. Nor does mass education constrain the resort to violence; in the information age modern weapons compete with box cutters, machetes and teen-age kamikazes in their power to annihilate. Nineteen men brought down the twin towers. In the aftermath of 9/11, we have a Department of Homeland Security with 185,000 employees and a $ 38 *billion* budget.

The modern American peace movement claims to oppose what it regards as a primitive reliance on violence to end violence. But there is more to the movement than that. It is a revolutionary complex that condemns western, *bourgeois* culture. This movement arose after World War I, flourished in opposition to the Vietnam War, and has been reconstituted to oppose America's war on terror. America's war resisters have created an ideological movement inspired by international revolutionary movements: Bolshevism, the Stalinist *International,* and the Third World movements begun by Ho Chi Minh, Mao Tse-tung, Fidel Castro, Kim Il-sung, Che Guevara and other models of provincial Communism. The leaders of this movement have nothing but disdain for the reasons why we need a U.S. Department of Defense and a Department of Homeland Security.

181

And yet at the same time, there is a uniquely American form of liberal or progressive anti-war dissent. It has roots in the Pilgrims, Quakers and abolitionists, and has been voiced by later generations of pragmatists, isolationists and free-traders who have protested war policies. I have tried to encompass the full scope of dissent in the text. However, it is important to emphasize that the modern ideological and political left is the principal force within the current anti-war resistance.

The literature of the comprehensive *whole* is readily available in most libraries. The following are among the most useful books. Many are overly sympathetic to the cause, but they are literate, colorful and informative:

Selig Adler, *The Isolationist Impulse: Its Twentieth Century Reaction,* (New York: Free Press, 1957).

Roland H. Bainton, *Christian Attitudes Toward War and Peace* (New York: Abingdon Press, 1960).

David Boulton (ed.), *Voices from the Crowd: Against the H-Bomb* (Philadelphia: Dufour Editions, 1964).

Vera Brittain, *The Rebel Passion: A Short History of Some Pioneer Peacemakers* (Nyack, N.Y.: Fellowship Publications, 1964).

Peter Brock, *Twentieth Century Pacifism* (New York: Van Nostrand Reinhold Co., 1970).

Patrick J. Buchanan, *A Republic, Not an Empire, Recovering America's Destiny* (Washington, D.C., Regnery & Co., 1999).

Grenville Clark, Louis B. Sohn, *World Peace Through World Law* (Cambridge, MA: Harvard University Press, 1958).

Wayne S. Cole, *America First: The Battle Against Intervention, 1940-1941* (Madison: University of Wisconsin Press, 1953).

Merle Curti, *Peace or War, The American Struggle, 1636-1936* (New York: W.W. Norton & Co., 1936).

Charles DeBenedetti, *The Peace Reform in American History* (Bloomington, Indiana University Press, 1980).

Allen Devere, *The Fight for Peace* (New York: The Macmillan Company, 1933).

John Dewey, *Liberalism and Social Action* (New York: G.P. Putnam's Sons, 1935).

G. Russell Evans, C. Gregg Singer, *The Church and the Sword* (Fletcher, N.C.: New Puritan Library, 1983).

Michael Ferber, Staughton Lynd, *The Resistance* (Boston: Beacon Press, 1971).

Louis Feuer, *The Conflict of Generations: The Character and Significance of Student Movements* (New York: Basic Books, 1969).

W. Freeman Galpin, *Pioneering for Peace, A Study of American Peace Efforts To 1846* (Syracuse, N.Y.: The Bardeen Press, 1933).

Adam Garfinkle, *Telltale Hearts, The Origins and Impact of The Vietnam Antiwar Movement* (New York: St. Martin's Press, 1995).

Robert Gilpin, *American Scientists and Nuclear Weapons Policy* (Princeton University Press. 1962).

Todd Gitlin, *The Sixties: Years of Hope, Days of Rage* (New York: Bantam Books, 1987).

Eric Goldman, *Rendezvous with Destiny: A History of Modern American Reform* (New York: Random House, 1962).

Arthur Herzog, The War-Peace Establishment (New York: Harper & Row, 1965).

Walter L. Hixson (ed.), *The United States and the Vietnam War: The Vietnam Antiwar Movement* (New York: Garland, 2000).

David Horowitz, *Unholy Alliance: Radical Islam and the American Left* (Washington, D.C. : Regnery, 2004).

Irving Howe, Lewis Coser, *The American Communist Party: A Critical History, 1919-1957* (Boston: Beacon Press, 1957).

Irving Howe (ed.), *A Dissenter's Guide to Foreign Policy* (New York: Frederick A. Praeger, Inc., 1968).

Paul Jacobs, Saul Landau (eds.), *The New Radicals* (New York: Random House, 1966).

Chalmers Johnson, *The Sorrows of Empire: Militarism, Secrecy and the End of the Republic* (New York: Metropolitan Books, 2004).

John B. Judis, *The Folly of Empire, What George W. Bush Could Learn from Theodore Roosevelt and Woodrow Wilson* (New York: Scribner, 2004).

Alexander Kendrick, *The Wound Within: America in the Vietnam Years,1945-1974* (Boston: Little Brown and Co., 1974).

Lawrence Lader, *Power on the Left, American Radical Movements Since 1946* (New York, W.W. Norton and Co., 1979).

Christopher Lasch, *The New Radicalism in America, 1889-1963: The Intellectual as a Social Type* (New York: Alfred A. Knopf, 1965).

Gunther Lewy, *The Cause That Failed, Communism in American Political Life* (New York: Oxford University Press, 1990).

——————— *Peace and Revolution ,The Moral Crisis of American Pacifism* (Grand Rapids: Eerdmans Publishing Co., 1988).

Alice Lynd (ed.), *We Won't Go* (Boston: Beacon Press, 1968).

Cord Meyer, *Peace or Anarchy* (Boston: Little Brown and Co, 1947).

David Mitrany, *A Working Peace System* (London: Royal Institute of International Affairs, 1943).

Scott Nearing, *United World: The Road to International Peace* (Mays Landing, N.J.: Open Road Press, 1944).

Reinhold Niebuhr, *Moral Man and Immoral Society* (New York: Charles Scribner's Sons, 1941).

Reinhold Niebuhr, *Christianity and Power Politics* (Scribner's, 1940).

William L. O'Neill, *A Better World, The Great Schism: Stalinism and the American Intellectuals* (New York: Simon & Schuster, 1982).

Harry and Bonaro Overstreet, *The War Called Peace: Khrushchev's Communism* (New York: W.W. Norton& Co., Inc. 1961).

S. Steven Powell, *Covert Cadre: Inside The Institute For Policy Studies* (Ottawa, Il: Greenhill Publishers, Inc. 1987).

Ronald Radosh, *Prophets On The Right, Profiles of Conservative Critics of American Globalism* (New York: Simon & Schuster, 1975).

Emery Reves, *The Anatomy of Peace* (New York: Harper & Brothers, 1945).

Melvin Small, *Covering Dissent* (New Brunswick: Rutgers University Press, 1994).

Matthew Stolz (ed.), *Politics of the New Left* (Beverly Hills, CA: Glencoe Press, 1971).

Robert Strausz-Hupe, *Democracy and Foreign Affairs* (New Brunswick, N.J.: Transaction Publishers, 1995).

Clarence K. Streit, *Union Now: A Proposal for a Federal Union of the Leading Democracies* (New York: Harper & Brothers, 1940).

George Weigel, John R. Langan, S.J. (eds.), *The American Search for Peace: Moral Reasoning, Religious Hope and National Security* (Washington, D.C.: Georgetown University Press, 1991).

Albert K. Weinberg, *Manifest Destiny* (Baltimore: The Johns Hopkins University Press, 1935).

William Appleman Williams, *The Tragedy of American Diplomacy,* (New York: Harper & Row, 1959).

Lawrence S. Wittner, *Rebels Against War* (Philadelphia, Temple University Press, 1984).

In addition to these selected works on the general topic, readers looking for contemporary insights into the anti-war movement, especially the Iraq occupation, should consult the following websites:

The Capital Research Center website, *capitalresearch.org,* contains a number of studies on the anti-war left (including my own); its monthly newsletters publish criticism of the left's most important nonprofit advocacy groups and philanthropic institutions.

David Horowitz's website, *frontpagemag.com,* assembles almost daily accounts of the internal workings of left-wing anti-war groups, replete with links to movement websites, eyewitness descriptions of demonstrations, and analyses by leading commentators. These include Ben Johnson, Robert Spenser, Ronald Radosh, Greg Yardley, Thomas Ryan, Michael Tremoglie, Anders G. Lewis, Stephen Schwartz, Dan Flynn, Jamie Glazov, Shawn Macomber, Anthony Gancarski, Edward Immier, Nick Cohen, John J. Ray, Steven C. Baker, Michael Radu and Peter Collier.

The Center for Security Policy, a Washington-based think tank led by Frank Gaffney, provides daily coverage of the most important news and commentary on security-related issues, including the activities of the anti-war left (*centerforsecuritypolicy.org*).

The website of *Insight* magazine (*insightmag.com*) ran a series of articles by J. Michael Waller on the anti-war network through mid-2004.

Incisive articles on the war against terror and its left-wing opposition appear in *National Review* magazine and its online website, *nationalreview.com*. The work of editors William F. Buckley, John O'Sullivan and Rich Lowry is complemented by the talents of Jonathan Adler, Jed Babbin, James Glassman, Ariel Cohen, Michael Ledeen, David Frum, Byron York, Michael Rubin, Victor Davis Hanson and Mackubin Owen.

Anti-war websites, left and right, provide valuable first-hand accounts of the motives, beliefs and activities of the groups discussed here. Besides the major groups (ANSWER, NION, UPJ), the following few will suffice to represent the spectrum of opinion:

The Institute for Policy Studies (IPS) has a daily site, *ips-dc.org*, which offers a thorough account of developments within the movement from an insider's perspective. Since 1963 IPS has been the Left's leading anti-war think-tank.

The Cato Institute (*cato.org*) and The Independent Review (*independent.org*) criticize U.S. foreign policies, including the war in Iraq, from a libertarian perspective. The Old Cause (*antiwar.com*) by Joseph R. Stromberg offers an ongoing series of anti-imperial essays based on often nostalgic recollections of American isolationism. Other libertarian, non-interventionist writers on this site include Paul Craig Roberts, Ivan Eland, Jim Lobe, Rep. Ron Paul, Jeet Heer, Laura Rozen and Dahr Jamail.

Of course periodicals are a leading source of information on the anti-war cause. It is sufficient to mention two: *The Nation*, edited by Victor Navasky, the oldest left-wing magazine in circulation, and Pat Buchanan's *The American Conservative*.

187

The following chapter notes identify quotations by reference to specific books and websites.

Preface, Introduction
Popper, *The Open Society and Its Enemies,* (Princeton University Press, 1966) p. 396.

Citations in the Introduction come from the website, *front-pagemag.com* or from the sites of the organizations quoted (e.g., ANSWER).

Chapter 1. Homefront
Todd Gitlin is cited in *San Jose Mercury*, October 28, 2001; "Who Will Lead?" *Mother Jones* (October 14, 2002); Interview with *Salon* (July 19, 2003).

The Communist Peace Offensive, A Campaign To Disarm and Defeat the United States, April 1, 1951, Committee on Un-American Activities, 82nd Congress, 1st Session, p.1.

The Worker's World Party And Its Front Organizations, Committee on Internal Security, House of Representatives, 93rd Congress, 1st Session, GPO, 1974, pp. 1, 6, 23, 24.
Quotations from antiwar groups come from their websites.

For assessments of MoveOn see the Capital Research Center newsletter *Organization Trends:* John Carlisle, "George Soros and MoveOn.org," (March 2004); also Peter Beinart, "A Fighting Faith," *New Republic* (December 13, 2004) and George Packer, "Smart-Mobbing the War," *New York Times Sunday Magazine* (March 9, 2003).

Chapter 2. Behind the Front Lines

For Gerald M. Steinberg, "The Thin Line Between Peace Education and Political Advocacy: Towards a Code of Conduct," a conference paper revised on February 22, 2004, see http://faculty.biu.ac.il/~steing/conflict/Papers/UNESCOPeaceStudies.pdf.

Herbert Romerstein is quoted in Michael Waller's article on the leftist movements in *Insight* magazine (March 4 – 17, 2003).

Quotes by Harrington and Heilbroner from Irving Howe (ed.), A *Dissenter's Guide to Foreign Policy* (see bibliography).

Material on anti-war groups and movement intellectuals can be searched in the files of *frontpagemag.com* under their names as well as at group websites.

Chapter 3. America's Manifest Destiny

Quotations on Manifest Destiny and the Philippine Insurrection are from *Manifest Destiny* by Albert K. Weinberg (see bibliography) and my own article on "small" wars in U.S. history, "America's Forgotten Wars: Guerrilla Campaigns in U.S. History," *Conflict* (vol. 2, 1980).

Material on the U.S. intervention in Nicaragua is from my Ph.D. dissertation (University of Pennsylvania, 1969) and article, "The United States and Nicaragua," *Orbis* (Winter 1971).

Chapter 4. Failed Peace Strategists

James and Dewey are quoted in Louis Menand, *The Metaphysical Club* (New York: Farrar, Straus & Giroux, 2001), pp. 361 – 363.

For Kennan on "legalistic-moralistic" foreign policy see his *American Diplomacy, 1900-1950* (University of Chicago Press, 1951), p. 95.

Strobe Talbott is quoted in *Time* (July 20, 1992).

For Ronald Radosh on conservative nationalism, see bibliography, p. 15.

The Senate hearing exchange on NATO is from Henry Kissinger, *Diplomacy* (New York: Touchstone, 1994), pp. 459-460.

The Jules Michelet quotation is from *La France devant l' Europe* (1871), which is cited in Robert Strausz-Hupe, et. al., *Building the Atlantic World* (New York: Harper & Row, 1963), p. 15.

Chapter 5. The Origins of the Anti-War Left
Lewy, (see bibliography), p. vii.

Evans, Singer, p. x.

Michael Walzer is quoted from his book *The Revolution of the Saints* (Cambridge: Harvard University Press, 1965), p. 317.

Suzanne Berger is quoted from her essay, "Politics and Antipolitics in Western Europe," *Daedelus* (Winter 1979), p. 32.

Feuer, *The Conflict of Generations,* pp. 407-412.

Mario Savio, *"An End to History,"* is quoted in Stolz, pp. 130-134.

Paul Potter, quoted in Garfinkle, p. 74.

See p. 267 of Garfinkle's book for his assessment of the anti-Vietnam war movement. See Kissinger, *Diplomacy*, p. 675 and George Kennan, *Democracy and the Student Left* (Boston: Little Brown, 1968), pp. 14-15 for their respective opinions of the anti-Vietnam War movement.

Statements by William Poole, Herbert Romerstein and Nguyen Minh from *Hearings Before the Committee On Internal Security,*

House of Representatives, 92nd Congress, 1st Session, June 15-17, 1971.

Final Reflections

John Lukacs, *The Passing of the Modern Age,* (New York: Harper & Row, 1970), p. 23.

George H. Sabine, *A History of Political Theory,* (New York: Holt, Rinehart & Winston, 1961), pp. 786-787.

194

202

205